They Call Me KILLER

They Call Me KILLER

*Tales from Junior Hockey's Legendary
Hall-of-Fame Coach*

Brian Kilrea and James Duthie

John Wiley & Sons Canada, Ltd.

Library and Archives Canada Cataloguing in Publication Data

Kilrea, Brian, 1934-
 They call me Killer : tales from junior hockey's legendary hall-of-fame coach / Brian Kilrea and James Duthie.

ISBN 978-0-470-67742-1

 1. Kilrea, Brian, 1934-. 2. Hockey coaches—Biography. I. Duthie, James (James F.) II. Title.

GV848.5.K55A3 2010   796.962'092   C2010-903732-4

Production Credits
Cover design: Ian Koo
Cover photo: Lynn Ball/Ottawa Citizen, Reprinted by permission.
Interior text design: Joanna Vieira
Typesetter: Thomson Digital
Printer: Friesens

John Wiley & Sons Canada, Ltd.
6045 Freemont Blvd.
Mississauga, Ontario
L5R 4J3

Printed in Canada

1 2 3 4 5 FP 14 13 12 11 10

To all of the players I have coached, my assistant coaches and trainers who were always in the background, but there for me, and the scouts, who continually supplied the Ottawa 67's with great talent and great kids.
—Brian Kilrea

To Mom and Dad for ... everything. And to Bill Patterson and Brian Smith, who introduced me to Killer and his great stories.
—James Duthie

Contents

Foreword

By Don Cherry

I was sitting in this bar, at the Empire Hotel, in Springfield, Mass. It was 1959. I was two years into my time with Eddie Shore in Springfield, the Siberia of hockey. I was miserable. Shore hated me. I was one of the guys who wouldn't argue with him, or suck up to him. I would just stare at him in my demented way. And he hated that.

So there's this new rookie on the team, and he looks about 13 years old. And he was sitting there in the Empire, saying how great he thought Shore was; how he thought he seemed like a wonderful coach. And I said, "If you say Shore is wonderful one more time, your head is going through that wall!"

That was the first time I met Brian Kilrea.

Outside of my family, I have had three great friends for my life: Whitey Smith, a paratrooper named Mel Price and Brian Kilrea.

I don't know why we hit it off back in Springfield. I guess we were the same. We were Irish; we liked having the odd drink, and a good time. And we were both rebels, I guess.

We didn't agree on Eddie Shore, that's for sure. Brian will tell you all the stories about that lunatic in this book, but no matter what he says, he loved Shore. I mean, Brian knew he was crazy, but he also thought he was a genius. Brian loved Shore, and Shore loved Brian. He skated and held his stick exactly the way Shore wanted his players to skate— knees bent, back straight. It was uncanny. And everything I did was the exact opposite of what Shore wanted!

Brian is the sharpest guy I ever met. That's why I always knew he was going to make a great coach.

One time, back in the Shore days, we were playing Euchre on the bus. I was always Brian's partner, and he carried me. He was the best Euchre player of all time. We were playing against Red Armstrong and Tom McCarthy. We played all the way from Rochester to Hershey, seven hours. We weren't foolin' around. This was serious stuff, dog eat dog. So we get there, and we're not done playin'. We say, "We'll meet you in Vince's Bar for the big showdown for $10."

Now, we got $4 a day in meal money. So think about it, a $10 card game was big money!

When I get there, Brian's already been there a while, and he's had two beers. I got really mad at him. I needed him to be sharp with $10 on the line! So we're playing for a while, and then Brian says to Red Armstrong, "You reneged. You had a heart." Red says, "No, I didn't!" Brian says, "Yes, you did. Third hand back. Count them." And, of course, he was right. He had caught Armstrong, and he wasn't going to say anything about it if we won, but we were losing, so he got him. So much for him not being sharp after the two beers. I yelled, "Another beer for Brian!"

It was the same with pool. He was so good at pool, when he was 15 (and he looked about 11), this guy would pick him up Saturday mornings and take him to the pool halls to hustle. He'd never lose.

Gerry Cheevers, the Boston Bruins and Rochester goalie, was really good at pool, too. He used to beat everybody. Gerry was a show-off. He'd put cigarettes between his teeth and stuff like that. When he beat you, he'd really rub it in. One time, when we were with Rochester, we were just sitting around watching Cheevers show off. I wanted Brian to play him, teach him a lesson. Finally, Cheevers asks him. Brian says, "I don't really play too much." Hustlin' him. So they play, and he lets Gerry beat him by one shot. Then they put up five bucks, and Brian runs the table! Never missed a shot!

Cheevers was steamin' mad. He looked at me, "You dirty ..." Because I had set it up, and I was laughing. Brian wouldn't have done that himself, but I wanted him to, just to get Gerry.

Brian was so good at pool that when he was playing junior in Hamilton, he was taking all the other guys' money. So Jimmy Skinner, the coach, calls him in and says, "What do you wanna be? You wanna be a pool player or a hockey player?"

Well, Brian wanted to be a hockey player. And you know what? I never saw him play pool again. And I'm telling you, he could have been a professional, he was so good.

He was a good hockey player, too. Never lost a face-off. Never. And he was a magician with the puck. He could dish it. Anyone who played on his line always ended up with 30 or 40 goals.

But he was a better coach. I knew that from the first time I brought him into my hockey schools. He put his heart and soul into it. And he was really tough. He could really give it to guys. People think he's all lovey-dovey because of the way he talks in interviews. Not true. He had no mercy.

One time we were doing the Prospects Game together, and as the guys were ready to come back on the ice, one guy, my first-round pick in Mississauga, went to take a piss, instead of doing it during the intermission like everybody else. Well, Brian just gave it to him! This was a Prospects Game! But he treated it just like any other game. There's no foolin' around.

If you did what you were told with Brian, you were fine. But if you were a wise guy, look out. He had this one guy in Ottawa who came in to see him, and he said, "I want to move. I don't like the lady I'm living with." So Brian said, "Okay, come back this afternoon."

So the kid comes back, and Brian says, "Well, I moved you." The kid says, "Where?"

"To Owen Sound."

He traded him!

Brian Kilrea is the best junior hockey coach of all time. And he would have been coach of the year in the NHL, if he had the chance. Just like me.

The other thing he's great at is tellin' stories. Brian is a storyteller deluxe. This book's a beauty, and I know you are gonna love it.

Preface

By James Duthie

I met Brian Kilrea on my very first day in this business. He was screaming. More like bellowing, actually.

It was winter, 1989. I was in my final year of journalism at Carleton University, and was starting a one-week work placement at CJOH, the local CTV station in Ottawa. We were supposed to be learning how to do television news that week, but all I really wanted to cover was sports. (I would end up getting hired by the station, and spending the first five years of my career as a news reporter there.) These were the days before TSN and the other sports networks were a big deal, so I had grown up getting my sports fix from Brian Smith and Bill Patterson, the two long-time CJOH sportscasters.

On that first day, which most interns spend fetching coffee for the staff, I begged Bill to let me tag along with him as he went to shoot a story on the Ottawa 67's, Killer's team.

I had followed the 67's since I was a kid. Every few Fridays, my Dad would take me down to the Ottawa Civic Centre to watch them. And come playoff time, I'd curl up in my captain's bed (don't giggle, captain's beds were very big when I was nine), listening to their games on the radio. I worshipped a defenceman named Steve Marengere. The team used to sell buttons with the players' faces on them. Marengere's mug lived on the collar of my ski jacket for three full winters.

Brian Kilrea was already an icon in Ottawa back then. The Senators hadn't been reborn yet, and the football team, the Rough Riders, was a little short on heroes (this tends to happen when you go 3-13 every season).

Killer was the city's best-known sports figure. I had watched him coach, and seen him countless times on TV, but I had never met the man until Bill led me into the Civic Centre that day.

I walk through the doors and hear this booming voice unleashing an endless stream of... err... colorful instructions ... to his players. Killer spots Bill and stops in mid-profanity. He skates right over and, smiling ear-to-ear, says "Hey, Billy! Whadya need today?"

He had gone from purple-faced tirade to cheerful greeting in a nanosecond. That was Killer, I'd soon realize. He hadn't really been angry. This was just the way he got his message across to the players.

He shook my hand that day, wished me well, told me I was learning from the best (which I was—Bill would become a mentor and dear friend), and went back to work.

"Move the puck! Move the puck! Move the !#*@in' puck!"

By the way, the use of those symbols from the top line of my keyboard represents one of the quandaries of this book. Killer, when he coached, was known for his Crayola-box use of language. If they ever film *The Brian Kilrea Story*, HBO will be the only TV option.

"I remember this one game we lost 7-2," says Brian Patafie, the 67's athletic trainer. "I came home and my wife asked, 'What did Killer say after the game?' I said, 'Do you want me to include all the expletives?' She said, 'No.' So I said, 'He didn't say anything.'

Thus, the odd word in this book will be altered or omitted. Or we'll use more of those helpful symbols (#*!), and you can use your imagination. When the word is truly necessary to tell the story, we'll leave it in.

I've been fortunate enough to know Brian Kilrea for my entire two decades in broadcasting and sports writing.

In 1995, Brian Smith, the Ottawa sportscaster who was also Killer's former teammate, was shot to death leaving our TV station. I moved into the sports department to replace him. It was a horrible time, and not the way I wanted to get my break in the business. From day one Killer told me not to worry about why I was there—just to relax, be myself and do the job. He would give similar advice to sportscaster Terry Marcotte a few years later when Terry replaced Bill Patterson, who died of a heart attack. Brian and Billy were the guys who first introduced me to Killer's great stories. They would tell them over and over, in their cubicles at the back of the newsroom, laughing louder every time.

I would end up interviewing Killer countless times during my stay in Ottawa. After moving to TSN, I'd call him every Christmas to get insight into the Ontario Hockey League players on Canada's World Junior Team. And we'd run into each other every November at the Hockey Hall of Fame Induction Ceremony.

When Killer was set to retire from coaching in the spring of 2009, we went to Ottawa to do a feature story on him for TSN. As the camera crew was setting up the lights and microphones, Killer started telling some of the tales about his playing and coaching days. I was falling off my stool. I figured it was time to get all the stories in a book.

This is that book. It is the result of hours spent in Killer's basement in Ottawa—just the two of us, the odd Molson Ex and a little red tape recorder.

My part was simple. I'd listen to his stories, transcribe them, and interview some of the other main characters. Their words will pop up, here and there, throughout the book.

This is not an autobiography. It is simply Killer telling tales, the same way he would if you sat with him in a bar for a couple of hours. Don't try to make sense out of the order of the chapters. Killer does not talk chronologically. He jumps back and forth between decades, between his playing and coaching days. The book will do the same.

I can't thank Brian and his wife Judy enough for their patience and hospitality during all those long interview sessions, and my countless phone calls that followed.

Brian Kilrea played professional hockey for 15 years, winning three Calder Cups and scoring the first goal in the history of the Los Angeles Kings. He coached the Ottawa 67's for 32 years, winning a record 1193 games, two Memorial Cups and four Canadian Hockey League Coach of the Year Awards. That award now bears his name.

Killer is one of the last true originals in the game. And his stories are classics. I know you'll have as much fun reading them, as I did listening.

James Duthie, 2010

1

They Call Me ... Gig?

Long before I was Killer, I was Gig.

When I was born in 1934, there was a comic strip in the paper with a baby named Giggles. Well, I guess I was a happy baby, always smiling and giggling, so my Mom and Dad called me Giggles. Pretty soon that was shortened to Giggy. And then it became Gig.

I was never Brian. I was always Gig. Even today, friends who have known me for a long time call me Gig.

I learned a lesson when I started coaching. People in the stands would yell, "Hey, Kilrea!" I'd look up and they'd usually say, "You're nothing but a no-good, lousy ..." You know where I'm going. So ever since, when someone yells my name, I don't look up. Unless they say, "Hey, Gig!" Then I look, because I know it's a friend.

When I was just out of junior, Detroit was going to send me to one of their farm teams in Troy, Ohio. Nellie Podolski was the coach and he was telling one of his best players, Stevie Gabor, that the team was getting this guy named "Kill-ree" or "Kill-ray" or "Kill-something." Stevie took one look at me and said to Nellie, "If that's the Killer you're getting, we're in trouble. That's one baby-faced Killer!"

That was it. From then on, I was Killer.

JD: *I guess we could have called the book* They Call Me Gig. *But that doesn't have quite the same ring, does it?*

2

Cigars, Anne Murray and Polar Bears

Move the puck!

I've been teaching them that since day one in coaching. When you have a guy open ahead of you, get it to him. Move the !*#&in' puck! It's pretty simple.

So this one night in 1990, we're playing at home and Chris Snell, a talented forward, gets the puck and has a guy wide open. But he decides to deke. He dekes one guy. Still won't pass. He dekes another guy. Won't pass. By now, the first guy he deked has come back and he hits Snell and steals the puck. Boom, boom, bing! They go up to the other end and score. It happens fast. Snell is still on the ice, and he's watched them put the puck in the net, so he stays down, writhing in pain. He's acting like he's really hurt, and that's why he lost the puck.

Our trainer goes to jump on the ice, and I stop him.

"Stay here," I say. "Let him be."

Snell keeps peeking over, but no one is coming. He's alone out there, in front of the whole crowd.

After a minute, the referee comes over and says, "You have a player down over there. Aren't you going to send your trainer out?" I say to the ref, "Nope. He's not hurt. If you want to go over and tell him to get off the ice, go ahead. Just let him know I'll be waiting for him here."

Finally, after a few minutes, Snell realizes no trainer is coming to help him. So he gingerly gets up and slowly skates to the bench like he's in agony. I say to Bert O'Brien, my assistant coach, "He stays on the bench."

Well, within a couple of minutes we get a power play. Now trust me, Chris Snell knows how to run a power play. He's always out there for us. He tells Bert he's okay, so Bert says, "Snell's ready to go."

I say, "That's good, Bert. You tell him he isn't going anywhere. I'll see him in the dressing room."

Let's just say Snell heard about it. Loudly. You don't come up with fictitious injuries and try to play the sympathy card on my hockey team.

Chris was a good kid and a good player. But he had to be taught a lesson that day. He learned. The hard way.

• • •

I coached hockey the same way for more than 30 years. I'm a pretty simple guy, really. I don't like change.

Like music, for example. I love Anne Murray. From day one, I just loved all of her songs. It started with "Snowbird," and "You Needed Me," and just went from there. I don't know all the names of the songs, but I could sing them all to you. Every word. I had one tape with all of her best on it that I played on every bus trip the 67's went on. When it would end, I'd just start it over again. I'd mix in some Nana Mouskouri once in a while, but mostly it was Anne Murray.

Oh sure, the players would get tired of it. You'd hear them from the back, "Not Anne Murray again! We're sick of this, Coach!" But I didn't care. Guys would try to play their own music. They'd put on the loudest heavy metal song they could find. Not a chance on my bus. I'd yell, "Turn it down or turn it off, those are your only choices!"

I bet there are a lot of former Ottawa 67's who know the words to every Anne Murray song—like it or not.

Andrew Cassels (Ottawa 67's forward, 1986–89): *As soon as that bus would leave the Civic Centre, this old 1980s boom box would start blaring his Anne Murray cassette tape. He would sit back with his cigar and sing along. When I was a rookie, I had to sit about three rows behind him. There was no escaping it. It was torture. Anne Murray still haunts me.*

Mike Peca (Ottawa 67's forward, 1991–94): *I didn't mind it too much. It reminded me of being at my grandmother's house.*

I guess Anne heard about me enjoying her music, because I got to meet her at one of her concerts at the National Arts Centre. What a thrill. I mean, Anne Murray meets kings and queens! She sent me an autographed book and signed a CD for my wife Judy. We still listen to the CD, but in the car. Now that I'm just a general manager, and off the bus trips, the players won't get the pleasure of nine hours of Anne Murray on the way to Sudbury. I'm sure they're pretty devastated about that.

I love cigars, too. After every win, I like to smoke a cigar. Okay, losses too. And ties, when we used to have ties.

I don't inhale, I just enjoy the taste. I smoke the Don Tomas #2 from Honduras. When I was playing in the States, you could never get Cubans, so Don Tomas is the one I stuck with. You can't smoke on the buses anymore, so I'd have one before I got on. Every single game. Like I said, I don't like change.

I enjoy a Molson or two after games as well. Though you can't bring beer on the buses anymore either. You see why I gave up coaching?!?

Back in the day, we'd measure the length of bus trips based on beer. Is this a six-pack trip? Or a 12? You didn't want to run out 50 miles before you hit town. My great friend Don Cherry invented the way to keep beer cold on buses when we played together in Springfield. He'd put it in a pillowcase and hang it out the window. Beer gets pretty cold on winter bus trips in the northeast. Don has made a lot of great contributions to hockey. That was one of his finest.

I don't have a lot of passions besides hockey, sports and my family. But I do love polar bears.

I saw a documentary when I was young, and I was fascinated. But I didn't have the desire to collect polar bear stuff until after I started playing hockey. First, someone gave me a picture. And then another one. Now I have polar bears all over my office down at the rink, and upstairs in the cupboards at my house.

What a great animal. They are so strong and fearless. I just respect them for surviving those tough northern conditions. Their little ones look like cute little puppies, and yet they grow to be so fearsome, so ferocious.

We went to Churchill, Manitoba, a few years ago, just to see them. We rode in a tundra buggy and saw 18 polar bears. They'd look up at you, but just walk on, absolutely fearless.

They are survivors. I guess I can relate to them. Hockey players have to be that way: tough survivour. Guys like Don (Cherry) and me, we were survivour. You play for Eddie Shore for eight years (you'll read about that later in the book), you have to be a survivor.

And there's no doubt, I like hockey players who are tough. As long as they're not dumb when they try to be tough.

We had a kid on the 67's named Mike Hodgins (1975–76). One night against Toronto, Mike took about four penalties in one period and they scored on three of them. So in the dressing room between periods, I walk in and I know I'm going to get him. But as a coach, my theory was always to yell at somebody else first or second, then get the guy you really wanted to get third or fourth. So I get on this guy and I get on that guy, and Mike is all pumped up, sitting on the edge of his seat, saying, "C'mon guys, we gotta get going out there! Let's go!" This is the guy who took all the penalties and got us down 4-1 in the first place!

I finally get to Mike, and he's all pumped up, and I say, "Guys, I want you all to look at Mike here. You see him? You see the passion and enthusiasm he's showing?" And now you can see Mike is excited even more because he thinks I'm about to praise him in front of the whole team. "You see Mike? Well, I tell you. He's only 17. And if he keeps this up, if he continues to improve, in three years from now ... (dramatic pause) ... He'll be 20!" And I walked out.

Well, the room just burst out laughing. Poor Mike, he thought he was The Man until that moment.

We came back and won that game, too. I've always found humour helps players relax. You can't keep going in that room period after period trying to give inspirational pep talks. If you keep telling them, "This is a huge period and you can't make any mistakes," they'll just keep making more mistakes.

I've always had fun with my players, but I have rules. And you don't want to break them, which brings me back to Mike.

We're having a practice one day and I'm explaining a forechecking drill we're about to do. I tell them I'm going to shoot the puck in, and have the defenceman go get it, and I want the forward to angle, so he's pushing the defenceman where you want him to go, so he runs out of space. As I'm talking and explaining this, Mike has his back turned to me, and starts talking to Doug Wilson, our star defenceman. Mike is a short, stocky guy and Doug is tall. So Doug is looking at me over Mike, and listening to me, not Mike.

So I say, "Hey, Mike, I guess you know what I want done in this drill?" He says, "Yeah, I know." So I shoot back, "Okay, why don't you demonstrate it for us. Doug, I'm going to shoot the puck in your corner and Mike, you go do what I told you guys to do."

I shoot the puck, Doug goes and gets it, and Mike goes in towards Doug then circles behind the net and comes right out in front and stops, looking at Doug from about 30 feet away! Doug is standing in the corner laughing, but I can tell all the other players are leery, wondering if I'm going to snap.

Well, I say, "Perfect, Mike! Great job! You have just demonstrated the exact opposite of what I wanted done!" Now I'm laughing, everyone is laughing, with one exception: Mike. He says, "I can't take this any longer, I'm getting out of here."

I say, "Mike, just cool down. You're the one who didn't listen. You are the guy who turned his back on me when I was talking, so just cool down and take it for what it is. You enlightened everyone."

But Mike wasn't cooling down. He says, "Yeah. Well, I'm leaving."

"Okay, Mike," I say. "But just understand this. The door swings one way. I'm going to suggest you skate around with the guys and settle down, because if you skate off, you aren't coming back."

Mike didn't take my advice. He skated off the ice and left. I continued with practice and, as soon as it was over, I called Orval Tessier, the coach of the Cornwall Royals.

"Orval, I know you've been trying to get Mike Hodgins for a while. If you still want him, you can have him. All I want back is what I drafted him for." Orval says, "Sounds good, you got a deal."

I try to call Mike at his house, but there is no answer. But a half hour later, I get a call in my office from Mike Buchanan, who is Mike's grandfather. Now, I knew Mr. Buchanan, and I liked him. I knew his two sons, who played hockey here in Ottawa at St. Mike's.

Mr. Buchanan says, "I hear you had a little trouble with Mike today. Well, I can guarantee you it won't happen again."

"Well, Mr. Buchanan, I can guarantee it, too, because I just traded him to Cornwall. When you see him, ask him to come and get his skates."

"Oh." (Long pause.)

The lesson had to be taught, so the next time my players heard, "That door swings one way," they listened and passed it on.

I liked Mike. In fact, he would call me later from Cornwall, promising to never say another word if I would get him back. As a matter of fact, he's still a friend of mine today.

I'm really not that much of a stickler with rules. I try to treat the players like men. But sometimes, you just have to make a statement.

Like I said, I'm a simple guy. Same music, same beer, same cigar, same polar bears, same rules. And I'm not going to change.

Mike Hodgins (Ottawa 67's forward, 1975–76): *The moment the words "fuck off" came out of my mouth, and I couldn't put them back in, I knew I was done. I could see it in Killer's face. I regretted it the second it happened.*

Truthfully, it killed my dream that day he traded me. Every kid has the dream. Every kid thinks they are going to be better than they are. When I got traded to Cornwall, I realized I wasn't special; I wasn't going to be a hockey player.

But he taught me a great lesson. And I use it to this day in my work. You're a team player or you're not. I wasn't a team player back then, and Killer did what was best for the 20 other guys on that team by getting rid of me.

Brian Kilrea was the fairest individual that I ever played for. He has a knack, if you allow it to happen, to teach you how to conduct the rest of your life. He doesn't give a shit if you're going to be a hockey player or a janitor or what you are going to be. The majority of his players become firemen or businessmen or something else. They don't become hockey players. He knew I wasn't going to be a hockey player. There have been 1,000 young men he's coached who he knew weren't going to play pro hockey. Yet he didn't treat them any differently than he did the Dougie Wilsons, Bobby Smiths or Peter Lees.

I wish people knew how much he did for people who didn't become hockey players. That, to me, is more a measure of the man than the 100 or so players he's sent to the NHL. If I went to his door tomorrow looking for help, I know he'd open it.

JD: *Mike Hodgins still lives in Ottawa. He is the finance manager for a large car dealership.*

3

Somewhere There's a Hero

We were heading down the corridor to our dressing room at the Ottawa Civic Centre when Matt Zultek pulled me aside. He says to me, "Coach, I'm so nervous. I'm just so nervous!" He was almost shaking. It was the end of the third period of the 1999 Memorial Cup Final. We had just blown a 4-1 lead against Calgary, right in our own rink, and were now tied 5-5. We were going to sudden-death overtime. One goal wins the biggest prize in junior hockey. So I say to Matt, "Listen, I'm nervous, too. Didn't you hear me on the bench? I called the name of a guy who hasn't played for me in two years! We're all nervous!"

It wasn't true. I didn't really call out some old player's name by mistake, though I used to do that a lot. I was just trying to calm the kid down. He was about to play the biggest period of hockey in his life. I couldn't have him scared.

When I went into the dressing room, the kids seemed okay. It was quiet, but they looked pretty confident. They weren't in shock or anything. I wasn't going to give them some big long speech. So I just looked at them and said, "Somewhere in this room, there's a hero."

And I walked out.

• • •

That was a special year. We knew we had a good team, and there was a lot of excitement in the city. It was the first year that Jeff Hunt owned the 67's. He bought the team off Howard [Darwin] and Earl [Montagano]. And we went from averaging 2,200 fans a game to 8,000 that year! Jeff's first game was a sellout.

He was amazing. He did a ton of promotion. He had an advertising budget that put other teams to shame. He went to every one of the papers, he put money into TV, into radio, he advertised everywhere. He said to me, "Killer, if I can't get them in the first year, I won't ever get them." Little did he know he was going to get a chance to win the Memorial Cup in his first year as an owner.

Jeff Hunt: *When I bought the 67's, the big worry I had was that Killer would leave. He was getting towards the twilight of his career and he had been with the same owners from the beginning. I figured he might say, "To heck with this new kid. I'm outta here!" So, one of my last conditions in the deal was that Killer had to stay. I told him, "If you don't stay, I have no credibility, so I won't do the deal without you." I asked him to do a three-year contract, told him I'd get it drawn up. He said, "I'll stay, but I don't want a contract. My word is enough." This made me really nervous. It wasn't the way I did business. But I quickly realized that's how he did business. A handshake was enough. So we've never had anything on paper. His word is more than good.*

I knew I had bought a good team. They had gone to the OHL finals that spring. But I remember vividly that summer, just weeks after I bought the team, picking up The Hockey News *and seeing the headline, "67's will win Memorial Cup." I thought, "Holy shit! I might really have something here!"*

The seeds of that team were planted at the draft three years before. The two big names in the draft were Joe Thornton and Nick Boynton. And we were drafting third. It was Barrie's first year in the league and they got the first pick, so everyone figured they would take Thornton, and then Boynton would go second to Sault Ste. Marie. So what happens? Barrie takes Daniel Tkachuk! That was a big shocker. He was a good hard-nosed guy, but he never did go pro. I turned to our guys and said, "We're going to get either Joe Thornton or Nick Boynton!" Sault Ste. Marie took Thornton, and Boynton was ours.

Bert O'Brien (Killer's best friend and longtime assistant coach): *Brian had been out scouting a lot that year and all he kept talking about was Nick Boynton. Boynton this, Boynton that, "I sure wish we could get Nick Boynton." Then all of a sudden the day of the draft: Bang! We get him. It was unbelievable!"*

And I loved Joe Thornton, too. But Boynton was just this big strong farm kid. And, boy, was he a leader. When he joined us, he was 16. But he was like a 21-year-old. I remember going to see him for the first time at his family farm in Nobleton. He was out in the fields working, and he just came in, signed his papers, and said, "Whatever you need, Coach," and then went right back out in the fields to work. I loved Boynton from the beginning.

We got lucky again at that draft. I had gone out scouting with Joe Rowley, our head scout, and he was showing me this guy and that guy. Well, I came back and said to Bert, "You gotta come back and see this one kid. I can't believe it! He skates with the puck and you just can't get it off of him. He looks like Bobby Orr."

It was Brian Campbell. He was playing for Whitey Stapleton in Strathroy, north of London. He wasn't the fastest skater but with the puck he became faster. Most guys, once they have the puck they don't skate as fast, but Campbell was one of those guys who went faster with the puck.

Anyway, we go to the draft and somebody starts a rumour: "Don't draft Campbell. He ain't going anywhere. He's not leaving home." There were a couple of teams spreading the rumour. Maybe they wanted to get him, I'm not sure. But they had a couple of chances and didn't take him. We were at the top of the third round. We took Boynton first, and because we got him, we took a flyer on a kid named Andrew Marek in the second round. There was some talk Marek was going to go to university instead, but we got him on the phone just before the draft and I said, "Do you want to be a hockey player?" And he said, "Yes!" So I said, "Would you give me a chance to talk to you about coming to Ottawa?" and he said "Yeah!" So we took him. As it turned out, his Mom and Dad, and I guess he, changed their minds. He went to school and never came to the 67's. Oh well.

Now we get to the third round and I say to myself, "Maybe we should have taken Campbell before." Anyway, we got him at the top of the third, and a couple of those teams who thought they were going to get him later said, "He's never going to go play in Ottawa." I shot back, "We'll see."

Brian Campbell (Ottawa 67's defenceman, 1995–99): *I didn't expect to go that early in the draft. In fact, my Dad was in the washroom when they called my name. I was sitting there going, "Is this really happening?" Ottawa was about the furthest place in the league away from my home, so I wasn't that keen on going.*

Before camp, Campbell goes to some under-17 camp down on the east coast, and he meets up with Nick Boynton at this camp. They bonded right away. And they would come right from that camp to our training camp. Campbell skated a couple of days with us, and then, one of our scouts, Patty Higgins, saw him leaving the rink with his equipment bag. He was going home.

Well, Brian and his parents come over to our house, and Brian isn't saying anything. His Dad is telling him, "Why don't you try it for a while, and if you aren't happy, come home." I could tell Brian wasn't so sure. He didn't want to stay. But then Nick Boynton calls and says, "I'll take care of him. I've already talked to my landlady and he can live with me if he wants." Nick helped convince Brian to stay.

Campbell was worried that he wasn't going to be good enough. You know what happened? He played the first exhibition game, and he was one of the stars of the game. He was 16 years old and he's out there having fun, skating with the puck doing this and that, doing everything! And after that, he was all right. He stuck it out and became a star.

Brian Campbell: *Killer just made me feel comfortable. I stood outside our bus after that first game in Belleville, said goodbye to my parents, and that was it. I realized pretty quickly this was the right place for me.*

Soupy (Campbell) was a key part of our run in '99. One night in Kingston, we had all sorts of injuries, and I was playing him a lot. His landlord had a stopwatch on him and he played 42 minutes of a 60-minute game! He told that story on *Hockey Night in Canada*. Remember when he played for Buffalo and they had all those injuries on their playoff run (2006)? The interviewer asked him: "You ever play that much before?" And Soupy said, "Yes, one night in Kingston I played 42 minutes!"

We didn't have anyone else. He stayed on the ice, we just alternated the guy beside him.

Bert O'Brien (Killer's assistant): *One year, we had the All-Star Game in Sarnia and we had to leave right after because we had to play in Windsor the next night. I kept using Campbell more and more, because even though it was just an All-Star Game, Killer and I still wanted to win. Wednesday night we played the All-Star, drove to Windsor, played Thursday night in Windsor, played Friday night in Sarnia, played Saturday afternoon in Plymouth, and played Sunday afternoon in London. Soupy played five games in five nights and he was logging 35 minutes a game!*

And he would just laugh and say, "I don't mind."

JD: *With Boynton and Campbell leading the way, the 67's rolled through the first half of the season. Meanwhile, the new owner was bidding to bring the Memorial Cup to Ottawa for the first time ever.*

Jeff Hunt: *I would have never done this with the experience I have today, but back then I was excited, and naïve. So the first night of the season, in front of a packed house, I did a speech at centre ice, and yelled, "We're going to win the Memorial Cup right here in Ottawa!" I'm sure people cringed, "Look at that rookie owner, making ridiculous predictions." We were bidding against some really tough competition. Then in January, I got the call from (Canadian Hockey League president) David Branch. He sounded all downcast, "Sorry, Jeff, bad news." I got mad. "Jesus Christ, Dave! Junior hockey was dead in this market! We've been doing so much to bring it back. We needed this!" He started laughing, "Jeff, I'm kidding. You guys won." He'd been messing with me!*

The team was on the ice practising, and I pulled Killer over to tell him. Then we told the team. The celebration was unreal. It was like they'd won game seven in overtime."

JD: *Hosting the Memorial Cup guarantees the 67's a spot in the four-team tournament. But they are determined to earn it, by winning the OHL title. They finish the regular season with the best record in the Canadian Hockey League. In the second round of the playoffs, they meet their archrivals, the Belleville Bulls. The 67's lead the best-of-five 2-1, and can wrap it up in Game 4 in Belleville.*

We had a couple of injuries, so we weren't at full strength. But we had a one-goal lead in the last minute. It looked good. The puck is behind their net with about 11 seconds to go, and they make a long pass and another pass, and they get the puck in front of the net, and suddenly it's in! They tied it up with three seconds left. And they won it in overtime. It was unreal.

Our guys couldn't recover. We lost Game 5 on home ice, and it was over. We were out, and all of a sudden we were faced with 40 days to prepare for the Memorial Cup. I sent them away for a week. I just said, "Get out of here. Go home and rest."

Bert O'Brien: *Smart move. They would have faced certain death if they stayed around that first week, with the humour Killer was in.*

Jeff Hunt: *Seeing Killer after the game, he looked devastated. I could see in his face that he felt he had let me down. So we went golfing the next day and I told him, "Our one goal is to win the Memorial Cup. And that's still our goal." It was one of the few times I gave him a pep talk. Usually it was the other way around.*

Getting beat was probably the best thing that could have happened to us. If we had to go through another tough series or two, with all the injuries we had, we would have been in big trouble. Because we had these 40 days off before the Memorial Cup, we got everybody healthy.

And, boy, did we work them. We did every drill I ever had to do when Eddie Shore coached me. I tried to change it up and do something different every day. We usually don't change an awful lot in practice. We skate, we pass the puck, we move it quick, we shoot the puck, we go up and down the ice. Simple. By doing those kinds of drills, they are always skating and it's game conditions. I don't believe in putting pylons on the ice. Though I've coached some pylons over the years!

I'd work them hard for five days then give them the weekend off, and say just be back in time for school on Monday. Finally, it got to the point where they were getting antsy. They wanted to hit. We had a couple of times where guys wanted to drop the gloves and go in practice. We had a guy, Bengt Gustafsson, a real tough kid who ended up being a police officer. He almost went a couple of times. That would have been a mistake for the other guy.

When it was finally time for the Memorial Cup, my guys looked ready.

Brian Campbell: *I remember the banquet before the tournament started. The other three teams all got up and left before dessert. We couldn't believe it. We were grabbing desserts from other tables, and feasting. What kind of teenagers leave before dessert? I guess they were just more uptight than us.*

We had to play the opening game of the Memorial Cup against Roberto Luongo and Acadie-Bathurst from the Quebec League. We had a bit of a scouting report on Luongo, to go high on him. He had a good glove, but wide, so if you get a chance: go high, but keep it close to his shoulder. That was the spot on him, from what we had seen.

So it turns out we get a penalty early in the game and Joe Talbot intercepts the pass and goes in on a breakaway. Boom! He goes right over Luongo's shoulder, just like we said! The first goal of the tournament is short-handed, and the guys just went wild. They were jacked up. We won 5-1.

Calgary was supposed to be the favorite. Pavel Brendl was their big scorer, and they had Brad Stuart on defence. Our game against them went back and forth until Dan Tessier scored in the last five minutes to give us a 4-3 win.

One more win and we were going straight to the final. It was Belleville again. After they knocked us out, they went on and won the OHL. So, here we go again.

We came out flying. We had them 4-0 after 14 minutes. And we lost 5-4 in double overtime!

That was tough. They knocked us out of the playoffs, and then they do that to us in the Memorial Cup, right in Ottawa. With the tiebreakers, Calgary made it straight through to the final. Acadie went 0-3 and they were out, so we'd have a sudden-death game to get to the final. Against guess who? Belleville, again.

That double overtime loss was a hard game, so I went to Nick Boynton, our captain, and said, "You want to give the guys a day off and just have a talk or do you want to skate?"

He said, no hesitation: "We're going to skate."

So, we skated on Friday, just to stay loose, do some drills ... 2 on 1s, 3 on 2s and the guys looked good. I had a good feeling.

The game was Saturday night at the Civic Centre and it had to be 80 degrees. You could feel the waves of heat every time someone skated by the bench. Belleville had chance after chance, but our goalie, Seamus Kotyk, was outstanding.

Seamus was a character in his own way. We always think of goalies being different. Well, Seamus loved to play bingo. You ever hear of another hockey player who loved to play bingo? Didn't bother me. Whatever makes you happy, as long as you stop the puck. I remember the next time we made the Memorial Cup, in Regina in 2001, a reporter asked Seamus what he was going to do with his off time. He said, "Maybe play bingo." Well, the whole city of Regina was offended, they thought he was making fun of them. But Seamus just loved bingo! They chanted "Bingo! Bingo!" whenever he made a save.

Seamus Kotyk (Ottawa 67's goalie, 1997–2001): *The funny thing was, before they interviewed me, some Ottawa reporters were interviewing Luke Sellers and he said, "I'd rather live at Jane and Finch [a rough area of Toronto] than Regina." Well, I was worried the Regina reporters might have heard that, so I was trying to soften things, by complimenting the nice bingo hall they had. I was serious, but they had this big headline saying I*

was making fun of their town! No one says a word about Luke's
comment, and the whole town's after me!

Anyway, back to 1999. Seamus stood on his head that
night, and we finally beat Belleville, 4-2. We were off to the
final to play Calgary again. Bingo!

But the heat and all the work caught up with Seamus. He
was dehydrated. Our team doctor sent him to the hospital.
We took the rest of the team to Chances R, our lucky restaurant, for some chicken and ribs and spaghetti. They were
all shook up, "Seamus is gone! What's wrong with Seamus?"
We didn't know what was going to happen. Here we were,
the night before the Memorial Cup Final, and our star goalie
was in the hospital.

It happened again the next year, too. We were playing in
Hull and he was standing in the crease and, all of a sudden,
he just went flop—face first on the ice. They rushed him to
the hospital. We were all scared it was a heart attack. They
did all these tests, and they found something wrong with his
heart. He had an operation and missed the last two months
of that season.

Seamus Kotyk: *I had a heart ablation, just like [Toronto Maple
Leaf goalie] Jonas Gustavsson had. They diagnosed it that night
before the Memorial Cup Final. But they said I was OK to
play. I didn't tell anyone. Killer was the kind of coach I never
wanted to let down. So, I would never tell him I was hurt. The*

next year, after passing out in Hull, I had the surgery and was out for the year.

So, we're all at the restaurant worried, when Seamus finally shows up. He was OK. We were good to go.

The final was Sunday afternoon. The electricity in the building was really something. Jeff had put up big screens in the Civic Centre salons next to the rink for all the people who couldn't get tickets. It was packed in there, too.

We got out to a 4-1 lead and were looking good. Then they got a couple of goals that Seamus should have had. Soon it was 4-4, and all the momentum was going their way. So I went to Levente Szuper, our backup.

And Szuper was great. All he let in was one power play goal the rest of regulation. We went up 5-4, then they tied it on that PP, and that was it. We were going to overtime in the Memorial Cup Final!

That's when Matt Zultek grabbed me in the corridor and told me he was just a bundle of nerves.

Poor Matt. The guys used to give him a hard time. He was such a big kid, he had trouble with his weight. He was 6-foot-4, and I would guess he weighed around 245. I told him once, "We'll have to take you to the stockyard to get you weighed!" We tried to put him on a diet, and he did shed some of it. He got himself into pretty good shape. But he was still a load. When he got the puck, you just couldn't move him.

Seamus Kotyk: *We always bugged Zultek about his weight. We called him Fat-tek and Ultra-tek. And WayneTub—that came from the fact he had his office behind the net, like Gretzky. It was a stupid nickname, but it stuck. I ran into him in Austria a while back, and the first thing I said was, "Hey, WayneTub!"*

So after I talked to Matt, I looked at the guys in the room and I didn't see any drained faces. I could tell they were ready to go out and get this over with. So I just said, "Somewhere in this room, there's a hero."

That was it. Didn't need to say anything else.

We sent Zultek's line (with Mark Bell and Justin Davis) out on the second shift of overtime. There was a whistle in Calgary's end, and they made a quick change. Maybe they thought we'd line match, I don't know. But we left Zultek's line on. The puck got down deep and came off the end boards. Zultek grabbed it, swept in and threw it on net. It went off the side of the goalie's mask and in.

The kid who was so nervous that he was shaking a few minutes ago had just won us the Memorial Cup.

I remember him jumping, but he was so big, he didn't get very far off the ice!

I saw the puck go in, but what I remember most was Vince Malette, our assistant coach, jumping from the bench to the top of the boards and leaping onto the ice. The goal was scored early in overtime and you know how slippery the ice is. He landed about six feet out on the ice!

Bert O'Brien: *He looked like Batman! I turned to Killer and said, "Where did he go?!?" Then he crawled back off the ice sheepishly, saying, "Did you see what I did?"*

They showed it over and over on TSN and all the sports shows, Vinny jumping. That's what I remember most about that moment.

Jeff Hunt: *I left my box and stood behind the [Calgary] net for overtime. I was a mess. The idea that we might lose the Memorial Cup at home in overtime made me sick to my stomach. And I kept worrying about the champagne. I bought a bunch of champagne, alcoholic and non-alcoholic for the underage kids, and was keeping it upstairs in a big fridge. I had to hide it because Killer is really superstitious and would have killed me if he knew I had it. I didn't know what to do. Bring it down to the room, so it's ready? But then what happens if we lose? It's amazing what your mind does in a situation like that. Then Matt scored and it was pandemonium. I remember seeing Killer do a double fist-pump. It was so rare for him to show elation behind the bench. I was so happy for him.*

It was unbelievable, winning the Memorial Cup in our town. In the dressing room, the guards couldn't control the crowds. They were storming down the corridor to our room like it was an exit. Fans were in our dressing room. We couldn't even get in. One guy was walking out with Szuper's mask!

Szuper was happier than anyone. He kept saying, "I'm the first Hungarian to win the Memorial Cup!" Seamus got us there, and Szuper picked 'em up. And Boynton was the MVP of the tournament.

They were so many heroes. Campbell was great. And Justin Davis led the whole tournament in scoring. Here's a guy who was going to be waived by the Soo the season before. So I called them and said, "I'll take Justin Davis. I'll give you a draft pick or the waiver money, whatever you want." I think we paid the waiver fee, $1,000, for him.

The boys were on such a high after we won, they didn't know what to do with themselves. So someone yelled, "Let's go jump in the canal!" The whole team went. They all ran across Bank Street in their red underwear and jumped in the Rideau Canal.

Seamus Kotyk: *The people by the canal looked at us like we were aliens when we jumped in. The whole night was insane. I remember at about 1:30 a.m., we were at this bar and the Cup was getting passed around all over the place. Jeff Hunt pulled me aside and said, "Take it home. Get it out of here." I think he was worried it was going to get lost or broken. So I took the Memorial Cup home. Nick Boynton called me in the morning, asking me if I knew where it was. They thought they'd lost it! I had to go downstairs just to make sure—the night had been a little foggy. But there it was, sitting on the kitchen table.*

Me, I was home by six. Jeff had me come over and speak to the fans in the salons who couldn't get into the game. So I spoke for a bit, and then I went home. I was exhausted. My wife Judy's Dad was there. He was well into his 80s, so we just cracked a beer and relaxed. It felt great. Then the phone rings. I pick it up, and it's Don (Cherry). He says, "What are you doing home, you should be out celebrating!" I said, "Don, I've been going every day ... I'm done." A couple of New York Islanders called, too—Bryan Trottier was one— just to say congratulations.

JD: *Killer left the 67's to spend two years as an assistant coach with the New York Islanders, before returning to junior hockey (see: Chapter 12: Long Nights on Long Island).*

That meant a lot. So I took those calls, sipped on a Molson, and I think I was in bed by 8:00.

But, trust me, I made up for it the next day!

JD: *Killer's two star defencemen that year, Brian Campbell and Nick Boynton, would be reunited 11 years later. Boynton was signed late in the 2009-2010 season by the Chicago Black-hawks, Campbell's team. They won the Stanley Cup together that spring.*

4

One Minute Between Legends

Detroit was always my team.

I had three uncles: Hec, Wally and Kenny. They all played for the Red Wings. Uncle Hec won the Stanley Cup in 1936, two years after I was born. But he was still there in the '40s when I was a kid, so I loved Detroit.

Back in those days, the paper wouldn't come until after 4:00, so I would race home from school every day to find out who had the goals and the assists from the game the night before. How many did Gordie get? How about Ted Lindsay? These guys were my idols.

I grew up, and became a decent player, and as it turns out, a Detroit scout named Alex Smart saw me in Ottawa and told Jimmy Skinner about me. Jimmy was coaching the Hamilton Tiger Cubs in the OHA. They were affiliated with the Red Wings. So they invited me to Hamilton for their training camp in 1953, and I made the team. And they ended up signing me to a contract.

JD: *Jimmy Skinner would coach Killer for one season in Hamilton before becoming head coach of the Detroit Red Wings. His Wings won the Stanley Cup the next year, 1955. Skinner is credited with starting the tradition of kissing the cup.*

So I belonged to the Red Wings, but I was still a long way from actually getting there. I spent two years in junior in Hamilton and then four years in Troy, Ohio, in the International League.

Troy's training camp was always in the same place as the Wings in Sault Ste. Marie, Michigan. When our practice was done, I'd hurry and get my gear off to go watch the Wings skate. They were amazing, like a machine.

During the season, we would play in Troy on Sunday afternoon, then I would drive the 180 miles to Detroit to watch the Red Wings play Sunday night. I loved that team.

My second year at that camp—I was 19—we were all just hanging around the hotel one day. Gordie Howe comes up to me and says he and Ted Lindsay are going down for an ice cream, and would I like to come along?

Would I like to come along?!? Cripes almighty, these guys were world champions and legends! Yes, I'd like to come along! So, we go get our ice cream, and then we come by a pool hall. Well, I had played a lot of pool as a kid. When I was about 14 in Ottawa, I would ride my bike uptown to this pool hall called The Little LaSalle, over the Centre Theatre. I was up there all the time, so I became pretty good at it.

Gordie says, "Let's have a game." It was Gordie and me against Ted and his partner, I can't remember who it was (I was a little distracted by the other two guys).

I held my own, and we won. Then we went back to the hotel, and now Gordie wants to play ping-pong. Well, it just happens that I had played a lot of ping-pong growing up, too. So Gordie and I won that game as well. It was just a fantastic day for a teenager to get to hang around these guys he idolized.

Ted Lindsay: *Gordie and I were living our dream, too. We were nobody special. So if we were driving to the rink, and the back seat was empty, and a kid like Brian was headed there, we'd pick him up. Or go get an ice cream, or shoot a game of pool. We liked to mingle with them, let them know they were part of the organization. We were no better than them. We were worried about making the team, too.*

JD (*Aside*): *Did Ted Lindsay just say he and Gordie Howe were worried about making the Red Wings every year? Wow. Sorry to interrupt. Carry on, Killer.*

The fact that I could walk around and say hello to Ted Lindsay and Gordie Howe—that was the highlight of my career. I didn't even care if I played a game with Detroit!

But I did. One game.

It was the 1957–58 season. I was still playing in Troy and the Red Wings had a couple of injuries. One of the guys hurt was Dutch Reibel, who played centre between Gordie and Ted. So they called me up. I was in the right place at the right time, I guess.

It was unbelievable. For a week, I got to practise with the Red Wings, playing centre between Gordie and Ted. They said, "Brian, just go to the net, we'll find you."

Dutch actually came back from his injury, but they still put me in the line up for a home game against Boston. I was nervous as heck. I just wanted to get dressed and look around the room at these guys. In warm-up, I mainly tried to stay out of everybody's way. These were all the guys I used to watch win Stanley Cups! And here I was, sitting on that bench next to them. It was unreal. I was glued to that bench most of the game.

But finally, they put me on. I was on the Detroit Red Wings, playing centre on a line with Gordie Howe and Ted Lindsay! I don't remember much about the shift, probably because I was just in awe, watching Gordie the whole time. It's pretty tough to focus on the opposition when all you want to do is watch Gordie Howe.

It was a pretty uneventful shift, but no harm was done. I didn't do anything dumb in my 40 or 50 seconds out there. I felt good about that.

But that was it. One shift. I spent the rest of the game on the bench. I remember it was 1-0 for Boston, and I was sitting near the end of the bench next to Beaver Poile. So Gordie comes over and says to me, "Touch this stick for luck, will ya." So I grabbed the stick and said to the stick, "Go get a goal!"

So what happens? Gordie goes out and scores! Then he comes back to the bench, looks at me and says, "You think you have another one?"

But the magic didn't work again. With the score 1-1, Don McKenney comes down the left wing for Boston, right in front of our bench. Al Arbour was playing defence for Detroit. Al stumbled a bit, and McKenney went by him and fired a slapshot. It caught the inside of the post on Terry Sawchuk and went in. Boston beat us 2-1.

The next day we got to practice and we're sitting in the room with all our equipment on, but no skates, just shoes. So Al Arbour comes in and Beaver Poile, who is a really funny guy, looks at Al's shoes and says, "Hey, Al, those look like the skates you had on yesterday on McKenney's goal!" Everybody broke up. Al did, too; he had a great sense of humor. It was a wonderful time, just being in the same room as those guys.

I was sent back down to Troy shortly after that. And I would never get back to Detroit. In fact, that one shift would be the last one I would get in the National Hockey League for eight-and-a-half years.

But what a memory.

I still idolize those guys. Jeff Hunt, the owner of the 67's, used to do a program where he would bring in the legends for our home games. I remember the night Ted came, and we sat outside and had a couple of beers. He was so kind to me. He gave me his number and said, "If you ever come my way, give me a call." I still feel the same way I did that day we went for ice cream when I was a teenager: just thrilled to be around these guys.

Ted Lindsay: *It is my privilege to know Brian. When you think of the thousands of players he influenced, and think of all the men he sent to the National Hockey League, it's amazing. I see him every year at the Hall of Fame now. It tells me volumes about the man. A lot of guys go in to the Hall, and never come back. I don't understand it. They think hockey owes them something. The truth is, we owe everything to hockey. Brian understands that.*

I'll never forget the night I ran into Gordie at the Hall of Fame ceremony a few years back. I was coming down the escalator to the main lobby, and Gordie happened to be coming up the escalator to the lobby, and we said hello and started chatting.

I was supposed to be taping an interview with one of those Toronto radio stations, and I knew someone was going to be looking for me. But I was not going to interrupt Gordie Howe. I didn't care if they had to wait an hour for me. He talked about Colleen and his kids and his dog. It was like he was just happy to be able to talk, not for an interview, but to someone from his past who really cared about what he was up to.

We must have talked for three-quarters of an hour. It was great. Then someone came and found him, and he had to go do some interview, and I had to go find my radio guy. But, man, was it ever wonderful spending time with the greatest hockey player ever.

I think he is. My friend Don Cherry says it's Bobby Orr, and what Wayne Gretzky did was unbelievable. But if you ask Wayne who the greatest player ever is, he says Gordie Howe.

To me, it's Gordie because he played in what was almost the same as the dead-ball era in baseball. The games back then were all 2-1, 3-2. They didn't have those 7-6, 8-5 games they had after hockey expanded and we went to 20-some, and then 30 teams. There weren't enough good players for 30 teams. There still aren't! Everybody had great teams when there were only six of them. And all six had an all-star calibre goalie.

So, for Gordie to amass the numbers he did, it was amazing. I mean, Bobby Orr would have been a star in that day, and Wayne Gretzky would have been a star. But would they have the same numbers Gordie Howe did? I don't think so.

When I talk to Gordie and Ted, I never ask them if they remember that one game, that one shift I played with them. I'm sure they don't. And it doesn't matter. I'm just honored they remember my name.

Ted Lindsay: *I don't remember the details of that game or that shift. But I remember the kid. And he did just fine.*

5

A Chance on Lance

One of the most satisfying things about my years in coaching is the chance to sometimes feel like you made a bit of a difference. When I think back about all the players who have come and gone, one of the most special is Lance Galbraith. Most people probably have never heard of him. But no 67's fan will ever forget him.

Lance was a good prospect coming out of bantam. He was a really tough kid, but he had a reputation. He had gotten in some trouble for stealing cars. It looked like he was headed for a juvenile detention centre.

He didn't even think he was going to get drafted. He showed up to the draft in Kitchener just to support some of his buddies who were going to get picked. I think he was wearing jeans and a T-shirt.

I liked what I'd seen from the kid, so we decided to take a flyer and pick him. So we announce his name, and he doesn't come down. We had seen him up there in the crowd, but we waited and waited and waited, and no Lance.

It was 45 minutes before he finally came down to our table. Turns out he ran back to change his clothes. His bantam coach was David Frost. Frost wouldn't let him come to the table until he was properly dressed.

Lance Galbraith (Ottawa 67's forward, 1996–2001): *I only showed up to see what the draft was all about, so I would be ready if I got drafted the next year. I was leaving when someone from the team stopped me, and said, "You better stay." I think I was wearing flip-flops or something. I ran outside and put on some cowboy boots, and fixed my hair. I couldn't believe it. They put this 67's sweater on me and said, "Make sure you give this back before you leave." But I was so excited, I left with it. That probably didn't get me off on the right foot. They take a chance on a guy who already had a rep, and he takes off with their jersey!*

After we drafted him, he had to go back to Brampton for his hearing. I wanted to help him out, so I wrote the presiding judge a letter. I told him if he could see his way to give Lance a chance, I would guarantee that I would bring him to Ottawa and take care of him. And I guess the judge took it to heart, because he gave him a suspended sentence. He gave Lance another shot.

Lance Galbraith would end up becoming one of the most popular guys ever to play for the Ottawa 67's.

He wasn't afraid of anyone. He would scrap with anybody, didn't matter how big they were. Anybody. Bert, my assistant coach, has a tape from 1996 of Lance when he was 16, fighting a 20-year-old kid named Andre Payette. He was one of the toughest guys in the league. It was on the *Global Game of the Week*. Sixteen, and he was fighting an over ager! And Lance wasn't real big. Didn't bother him at all.

The fans loved him. Lance would hit everything. He had this way of going into the corner to get someone in a straight line, and if he missed, he was like a bug on a windshield. The fans would be all upset, "Oh, my God, Lance is hurt. Poor Lance!" He'd limp to the bench and go, "I'm OK, Coach, put me back in." Only his pride was hurt because he missed the guy.

But Lance was a real test for me. Yeah, there might have been a late curfew ... or a few. We'd have it out regularly. But I couldn't have traded him even if I wanted to. I had promised that judge I would look after him, and if I traded him, I couldn't look after him. Of course, I could never tell that to Lance because, boy, then he could have really made it tough on me!

Seamus Kotyk (Ottawa 67's goalie, 1997–2001): *Killer had a soft spot for Lance, but he would always give it to him. I remember one game Killer was screaming Lance's name to get off the ice. He must have yelled, "Lance, get off!" three times. Then on cue, like a movie, Lance turns around on the bench and yells back, "I'm sitting right in front of you!"*

Lance Galbraith: *He went after me pretty good. I slid into Killer at practice one time and knocked him down. He looks at me and says, "Either you are going to kill me, or I'm gonna kill you!"*

I knew Lance was a good kid at heart. And, boy, did his teammates love him. One time, in his rookie year when he was 16, he missed curfew and I sat him out for a game. So, he doesn't play, and we lose by a goal. After the game, we are walking to the dressing room and one of the most respected guys in the room, David Bell, who was an over-ager, says to me, "Coach, why didn't you have Lance in the line up?" I told him, "David, you gotta have rules." And David, who was this quiet leader who never really spoke up about anything, says, "Yeah, Coach, but we're a lot better when Lance is playing." That's a 20-year-old begging for a 16-year-old to play. That says something.

Lance was a character. He could poke fun at himself. One time, we drove into Oshawa for a game, and we see this brand new van that Oshawa has bought, and on the side of the van is a picture taken from the newspaper. And it's Lance, standing over the Oshawa goalie, who has the puck. It was an action picture of their team, but it happens to be Lance in the picture, and it's big and you can see "Galbraith" plain as day on the back of the sweater. So, Lance is at the back of the bus, and we call him up and say, "Lance, you gotta see this, you're on the Generals van!"

Lance comes running up and says, "Would you believe that? I used to steal those things and now I'm on the side of 'em!"

Bert O'Brien (Brian's long-time assistant coach): *Another time, a bunch of guys showed up for practice in a cab. And Killer is screaming at them because they are supposed to car pool, and this taxi has cost 40 or 50 bucks, so Killer is really upset and is tearing a strip off of them, and then Lance says, "If we don't have enough cars, Coach, I can probably get us some." That cracked everyone up. He really knew how to poke fun at his past.*

I remember when he came back and joined us as an over-age player. We didn't know he was coming back until late, and he joined us partway through training camp. So, in walks Lance and all the guys are really happy because they love him. They know Lance is tough, and he's a winner, so they're excited to have him back.

I had talked to my friends down the street, Grace and Ted Cunliff, five doors down, who boarded a lot of players for me. I told them Lance was a little headstrong, but asked if they would take him, and they said, "Sure, we'll take him." So I told them he'd be there after practice that night to move in. I said to Lance, "You want me to take you there?" He said, "No, Coach, I'll get one of the guys to drive me over."

So it's all set up. Lance is going to Ted's. No problem. Well, the next morning Ted calls and says, "Killer, I thought Lance was coming to live with us?"

I said, "He never showed up?" Ted said, "No, we were up all night waiting for him."

Well, I was calm with Ted, but I was fuming on the inside. I told Ted that Lance was probably out with the boys celebrating his return and they probably didn't want to drive, so he must have stayed with one of them. I promised Ted that Lance would be there that night.

So I waited in the corridor as the guys came in for practice, and I stopped Lance and said, "Hey, Lance, how did you enjoy Grace and Ted's last night?"

He says, "Oh, they're really great, Coach. They're really super people. I'm going to like it there."

I had him good. I said, "You liar, you didn't even go home last night!" Then he got all quiet and embarrassed and said, "Yeah, sorry, Coach, we had a few and … you know … I promise I'll go tonight."

I said, "You're going all right 'cause I'm taking you there!" So Lance got a little escort to Grace and Ted's place that night.

Lance Galbraith: *Oh, did he go off that day. There was smoke coming out of his ears. I was thinking, "Oh My God, it's my first day back, and I've screwed up this bad already." But I apologized to him, and to Grace and Ted, and it was another lesson for me.*

But mostly, Lance stayed out of trouble. And all he did was win. Do you know he's played more playoff games in the history of the 67's than anyone? He wins a Memorial Cup, goes to another one. Then as a pro, he goes to Idaho and wins two championships there. The guy plays to win, and that's why all his teammates love him, wherever he plays.

Up in our dressing room are the pictures of the players whose sweaters have been retired by the team. There's only three: Doug Wilson, Bobby Smith and Denis Potvin. That's pretty select company. And our fans went after us because they wanted to retire Lance's sweater! They voted for it. I didn't do it. I couldn't put him with that group. But he did a lot for our team, and he left, I think, a better man.

When it was over, he didn't really say goodbye, because we all knew he'd be back. Even last year, he showed up at our first game in Brampton, just to say hello. He's a super kid.

I'm glad I wrote that judge the letter. I'm glad I got a chance to coach Lance Galbraith.

JD: *Lance is now 29, and still playing professional hockey. At the time of writing, he had just signed with the Wichita Thunder of the Central League. He still fights, though he tries to choose his opponents a little more wisely than when he was 16. He calls his time with the 67's the five best years of his life.*

Lance Galbraith: *I don't even like to think about what my life would have become if Killer hadn't taken a chance on me. If I'd kept going down the path I was on, it scares me to think where I would be. My entire life changed that day at the draft. It turned me around forever. I've played nine years pro, I've been able to turn this into a job, and I feel lucky every day.*

Killer leaned on me extra hard. And I'm so grateful for it. He taught me about respect. He became a father figure. I'm still trying to pay him back by bringing the same heart and soul to the rink that he coached with every day.

6

Life in Hell with Eddie Shore

JD: *Killer's stories about the legendary Eddie Shore read like a bizarre Shakespearean comedy/tragedy. Except it's set in Springfield, Massachusetts, in the 1960s.*

Act 1—Owned by Crazy Eddie

Eddie Shore. Where do I start?

How about the time he put a rope over the crossbar, like a noose, and put it around the neck of his goalie, Bob Senior. They called Bob, The Ox. Eddie was trying to stop him from going down too fast on shots. I guess almost hanging a guy was Eddie's way to get the message across.

I ended up playing for Eddie Shore because he happened to be standing in a hotel lobby one night at exactly the right time.

It was 1959, and I had been playing with the Troy (Ohio) Bruins, in the Detroit system. They were going to move to Greensborough, North Carolina, the next season, to play in the Eastern League. Well, there was no way I was going to Greensborough. My Mom and Dad were getting up in age, and I didn't want to go any further away than the northern States. Greensborough could have been on the other side of the world in my pea brain.

So I wrote the team in Fort Wayne, Indiana, saying I'd be interested in staying in the International League and playing with them. I figured Fort Wayne was easy enough to get to.

It wasn't just geography that had me looking to move. In Troy, they had this owner named Ken Wilson. My last year there, the players voted on the Most Valuable Player Award, and I won. It was nice, because the winner got a diamond ring. Well, I had also won the year before. So, Ken Wilson is presenting the award, and he says, "It was a close vote, so I'm going to give the MVP to Andy Millen." I was peed off. The players all told me they voted for me. I was the leading scorer, the guy killing penalties, the guy winning face-offs. Andy was a real good player, but hey, a diamond ring was something back then, so I was really mad. When it was announced at our last home game that Andy won, some of the crowd booed.

I hadn't turned pro yet, so I could sign with whomever I wanted. I was mad at Ken Wilson, and I didn't want to go to Greensborough with his team. So, I went to Eddie Shore's camp in Niagara Falls.

Shore ran the Springfield Indians in the American Hockey League. He was known as a tyrant. But I went to his camp and played pretty well. So Eddie offered me a contract. It was $4,000 for the year and a $2,000 bonus to sign.

Now, everyone told me, I mean EVERYONE: "Whatever you do, don't sign with Eddie Shore! He's crazy!" I mean I heard every negative adjective you can imagine to describe Eddie Shore. Over and over again, all I heard was, "Killer, whatever you do, don't sign with Eddie Shore."

So I didn't exactly jump at his contract offer.

It turns out Ken Wilson, the guy who stole my MVP ring, was also in town looking for players, along with his coach, Rollie McLenahan. They asked me to have dinner with them. Ken Wilson says, "We want to offer you a contract to come play in Greensborough, and we'll pay you $3,500 for the season."

So I say, "Well, Ken, remember in Troy when I was the best player and MVP but you didn't give me the ring? Well, sorry, I'm not going to sign with you."

Wilson gets real mad. He says, "You didn't need two rings." I say, "That's your opinion." So Wilson says, "If you are going to bring that up, if that's the way you are going to be, I know you wrote that letter to Fort Wayne. Guess what? You will never end up in Fort Wayne. I'll make sure of that!"

I had heard enough. "Good," I told him. "Don't worry, because I'll never end up with you in Greensborough, either." And I got up and walked out of the restaurant.

I was steaming. I walk back into the Foxhead Hotel, and who is standing there in the lobby? Eddie Shore. Eddie says, "Hey there, you thought anymore about that contract offer?"

I said, "As a matter of fact, yeah. Where do I sign?"

I think Eddie was caught a little off guard, but he said, "Come with me."

So we went upstairs to his room, and he pulls out all these papers, but he hasn't filled out the contract yet. I said, "I don't care. You told me what you'd pay me, so I'll sign it and you can fill it in after."

Eddie was startled. He said, "That's the way you do business?" I told him my word was good, and I trusted him. So I signed a blank contract to turn pro, and play with Eddie Shore in Springfield.

Well, the next morning there's a knock on my door at 7:00 in the morning. It's Rollie McLenahan, Ken Wilson's coach in Greensborough. Rollie says, "Ken's going to pay you $4,500 to play with us." I said, "Too late. I turned pro last night with Eddie Shore. Tell Ken Wilson to give the contract to the guy he gave my ring to."

Eddie was something. He was already running the team in Springfield while he was still playing with the Boston Bruins. When his playing days were done, he just ran Springfield. When I got there, his team was affiliated with the New York Rangers. But only the affiliated players could go up and down. The rest of us were owned by Eddie. And, boy, did he own us.

He controlled everything. The contracts, the suspensions, who played, who didn't play. It was all Eddie. Pat Egan was his coach, but Eddie ran all the drills at practice. He would stand on the bench at centre ice and do all the correcting, all the scolding, everything.

As soon as I got there, he decided he was going to change my game. When it came to skating, Eddie wanted your hands the width of your body. He wanted you to sit in a crouch, and have your elbows in. So one day at the end of practice, after everybody else was off the ice, he put a skate lace around my elbows and tied it at the back. He taped my gloves to my stick so that I couldn't reach for a pass. He put a lace around my legs so I couldn't take a long stride. Then he put a stick up my back so I was straight up and down.

I was a choppy skater so I actually got a ways with all these things tied to me. So I'm skating around the rink and I'm doing pretty good, and then he yells, "Turn!" I was somehow able to do that all right a couple of times, and I could tell he was getting really pissed off that I wasn't falling down. He started yelling, "Turn!" every two seconds. With all those laces tied around me, I couldn't turn that fast, so finally I fell.

The New Haven team was waiting to get on the ice. They had a lot of guys I'd played with in the International League—Gordie Stratton, Don Berry—and they were all watching. So, now I was embarrassed and fed up. I picked myself up, ripped my gloves off my stick, threw the stick into the stands and yelled, "Shove it!"

Eddie says, "Hey, you're just getting it! Now go get your stick and get in the room."

Denny Olson (Springfield Indians forward, 1958–65): *Eddie would say, "I want you to skate like a Boy Scout taking a shit in the woods. You gotta position your back so you don't shit on your heels!"*

My time with Eddie was almost over before it started. The first game I ever played in Springfield, I scored a goal. The team left for a road trip after the game, but Eddie kept me home. The next weekend we had two more home games, and I scored a goal in each. Then the team goes back on the road, and he leaves me home again. So I got angry and told him, "If I'm not good enough to play road games, I'm not good enough to play in this league! So trade me!"

I took my skates and went home. I told my wife, "Judy, let's go to the bank and get our money and get out of here."

But Eddie sent his trainer, Jack Butterfield, over to my place. Jack convinced me to ride it out. So I did. And what a ride it was.

Eddie was one-of-a-kind. Sometimes he brought the Shriner Circus to the arena, and if you weren't playing that night, you'd be out selling programs. Like I said, he owned us. One of his punishments was having players run around this horse track behind the arena. Once, he was trying to get the late Bruce Gamble to drop a few pounds. He made Bruce run around the track and he followed him in his car, yelling at him the whole way.

Bill White (Springfield Indians, defenceman, 1962–67): *Eddie was so meticulous about his ice. The Zamboni would go over it, then Eddie would walk out with a watering can and fill every hole. Well, I was chewing tobacco back then, and I would spit it all over the ice. He couldn't figure out all these spots on his perfect ice. I said, "Eddie, you must have a leak in your roof." Finally, on a road trip, he called me up to the front of the bus. He said, "Mr. White, from now on, I am going to fine you $25 for every spot I find on my ice." I spit over the boards from then on.*

Shore also thought he was some kind of chiropractor. He always wanted to crack your neck or your back. He messed up Barclay Plager's back one time. Barclay had to go to a real chiropractor to get straightened out again.

One time, he called me down to the rink late at night. I was excited. I thought he traded me, and I was going to be free from Springfield. Instead, he says, "Get on the table, I'm going to crack your back." Well, there was no way I was getting on that table. I said, "There's nothing wrong with my back!" And I left.

The next day, he took me out of the line up because I hadn't let him crack my back. The trainer told me, "He'll put you back in if you let him crack it." So I did. He cracked me, and twisted my hips and contorted me all sorts of ways. I had to have a spinal fusion years later. I blame Shore for that!

Before a game one night, he was twisting the neck of our goalie, Jacques Caron, all over the place. Jacques was sitting on a chair, and Eddie kept pulling his head upwards. Well, Denny Olson was watching all of this, and he says. "Hey, Ed, one of those things ever come off in your hands?" The whole room was trying not to bust up. I think Denny got one shift that night, and then he was made a black ace.

Denny Olson: *Shore had hands like a gorilla, and big thick fingers. They were so big, he had trouble doing up his laces. That night, Jacques had a bad cold, and Eddie believed snapping a guy's neck would cure a cold. I couldn't stop myself. It really looked like that head might come off!*

Jacques got in a fistfight with Eddie once. Jacques's wife had come to see us play one night in Buffalo. We won the game, but Eddie said, "No wives in the players' rooms." Caron was really mad. His wife was recovering from an operation, and he was really looking forward to spending some time with her. Anyway, they started arguing, and Jacques said, "You don't scare me, old man." Eddie shot back, "Come into the dressing room and we'll see who's an old man." And the next thing you know, they are going at it. I'm not sure who won. There was about a 40-year age difference, but it didn't matter. Eddie was strong and tough.

I ended up getting suspended because of that fight. After the fight, Jacques told me and Barclay Plager that he'd been suspended and fined $500. I told him to get a lawyer, because I had heard Eddie threaten him. Well, Al Murray was our coach then, and I guess he overheard this and told Shore, because in the middle of the night, Al knocks on my door. He was sending Barclay and me back to Springfield on the 5 a.m. bus. You weren't allowed to be a witness against Eddie Shore.

I was captain in Springfield for a while. One year, Wayne Larkin was on my line and he had a bonus in his contract if he scored 20 goals. Well, we had a good line and we were clicking. Wayne was getting goal after goal after goal. So, what does Eddie do? He benches him to stop him from scoring 20.

I was mad. I went to Shore and said, "Why would you take Wayne off our line?" Eddie didn't give me an answer. He just said, "You're no longer the captain of this team." And he stripped me of the "C," right then and there.

Denny Olson: *Here's one Killer never lets me forget. We were in camp in Hamilton, and my wife was coming in from Kenora, so I met her and my kids in Toronto. I had a quiet night with my family and was asleep by 11:00. Turns out the rest of the team decides to have a little party. Shore heard about it, and he sends up three cases of beer and a bottle of whisky. Nice guy, right? Well, the next morning he skates us to death! Stops and starts, starts and stops, endlessly. Everyone on the team, including Killer, is leaning over the boards getting sick. And I'm dancing out there. One of the spare goalies was a friend of Shore, and he had squealed about the party. So Shore sent up the booze just so he could make us pay the next day. Teddy Harris punched that goalie in the eye.*

Christmas was shortly after that, and one day Shore brought two cases of beer into the dressing room and said, "Here's your Christmas present." Roger Cote, one of our teammates, said, "I wouldn't take another drink off you if you poured it down my throat!"

Act 2—No Escaping Eddie

The only time we ever got away from Eddie was on the road. Usually, he wouldn't go on road trips.

One day, we were supposed to be leaving for a road trip to Pittsburgh at 2:00, right after our practice. But then at the last minute, Eddie changes it and decides we're not leaving until 4:00. So, some of the guys got off the bus to go get lunch. The rest of us stayed and played cards. Then Eddie suddenly gets on the bus and says, "I want the bus to leave right now!"

"But a bunch of the players aren't here," we told him.

"I don't care, get this bus moving now!" he yells.

We weren't sure what to do, so we left one guy back, and drove off—but we parked the bus a couple of blocks away to wait for the other guys. Somehow, Eddie found out. He sent his son Teddy over to tell us we had to leave right now, without the other players.

So we left again, and this time we parked right at the entrance to the Mass Pike (Massachusetts Turnpike) to wait for the other players. We finally got them back on, and were able to take a full team on the trip. I still have no idea why he did it. He was just mad about something.

Another time, we drive from Springfield to some crappy motel in the middle on nowhere. We don't get there till midnight. Next day, we have to get up and drive to Pittsburgh to play that night, a Wednesday. After the game, we get back on the bus and drive back to that same motel in that small town. Then we drive all the way back to Springfield and don't get back until 8:30 at night on Thursday. Now we have to play Friday and Saturday in Springfield, and Sunday in Providence. That's four games in five nights with a massive amount of driving. But we had a good team, a great bunch of guys, and we end up winning three of the four games.

So we get back really late from Providence, after 1 a.m., and we were all expecting to have Monday off. But as we're putting our gear in the room, Pat Egan, the coach, writes on the board: "Everybody on ice, 8 a.m. And regular practice, noon."

After that killer week, we were basically going to be at the rink all day!

Well, you can imagine our reaction. I say, "Pat, is this correct, what you have on the board?" He says, "Yes, it is." So, I run out and get Sam Pompei and Eugene McCormick, the two reporters who covered our team. I say, "You guys should come in here and see this. You want to write about the great man, Eddie Shore? Well, this is what he thinks of his team!"

I was steaming. We decide there is no use going to bed. We had a pal with an extended-hours bar called The Empire. He left the kitchen and the bar open for us, and we went straight there. You could get a soup or a salad ... or something else. Needless to say, we all went for the "something else." Plenty of the something else!

We headed back to the rink around 6:30 a.m. Most of the guys hadn't changed. This was probably the first 8 a.m. practice in history where all the guys were in shirts and ties. We hadn't changed since we left Providence.

Well, that was the day I found out you can't skate backwards if you've had one too many. We had one guy who just kept falling. It was a pretty ugly practice. You could really smell the beer perfume. After the early morning skate, we left our gear on and went over for a bowl of soup across the street. The newspapers were out. The two reporters had both written articles about how unfair it was to put us on the ice that early after all the travel.

We get back on the ice for the second practice, and Eddie walks in. He has this habit of twirling his whistle really slowly, especially when he's mad. He stands at his spot on the red line and twirls that whistle. And he would exercise his jaw by lengthening it out. So he's twirling and stretching his jaw, and staring at me. You could see the froth forming around his mouth.

He points at me and yells, "Are you responsible for that article in the paper?"

I couldn't help myself. I say, "What article? I had to be here so early, I beat the paper boy to my door! I haven't seen any paper. What did it say?"

Now, he was really fuming. He sent me to the corner, and made me do stops and starts for the entire two-hour practice. A lot of the time, guys dog it when they have to do those. But I was so mad, I kept cutting as hard as I could. I wanted to take that ice down to the pipes. I was cutting up the ice so bad, he finally had to send me to a corner at the other end of the rink.

The punishment wasn't over. For the next three days, he took me off my line. I was a black ace. That was Eddie's way, he always wanted you to know he was the boss.

Denny Olson: *One Christmas Eve, Eddie scheduled a practice at 8:00 in the morning. We thought, "Great, we'll have most of the day off to get ready for Christmas." I had family coming over for the day, so I was excited. So we get to the rink at 7:00, practice for 90 minutes, and then he says, "Back on the ice at 10:00." Well, we ended up having four practices on Christmas Eve! I got to the rink at 7:00 and left after 5:00!*

On another road trip, we were in Baltimore on a Tuesday and Hershey on a Wednesday. We always looked forward to Hershey because there were a couple of good bars there that really catered to us. The food was always good and the draft was always cold. The game in Baltimore was at 7:00, so we knew we'd be in Hershey early enough to have a good night out.

But, as we're skating around in warm-up, I suddenly spot Shore, with his big hat, up in the crowd. He had decided to join us on the trip. I said, "Uh oh, boys, Eddie dropped in to say hello."

Remember that style of skating I told you Eddie wanted everyone to have, with their knees bent? Well, immediately, everybody changed their warm-up to that style because they knew he was watching.

Now, before I get to what Eddie did to us that night, one more story about that day. Denny Olson and I were good buddies, and we went to a movie that afternoon in Baltimore, to relax before the game. It was *Days of Wine and Roses*, with Jack Lemmon and Lee Remick. Great movie. He becomes an alcoholic, then later she does, and he has to stop drinking to stop her. It was a really impressive movie. Lemmon was nominated for an Academy Award.

So, we're leaving the theatre and Denny says, "When's the last time you went a night without a beer?"

I said, "A long time."

He says, "Me, too. Let's see if we can do it just to prove we can."

Bad idea. At least that night. Baltimore had a hot rink. With about three minutes to go, we had a one-goal lead. Then our line scores a goal, and another, and we know it's over. Well, with about a minute to go, I come off the ice and I'm sweating and puffing. It is so hot in there. I look down the bench at Denny, and he's looking at me, and he says, "You know that little bet we made? It's off!"

I said, "Good!"

Denny Olsen: *So much for* Days of Wine and Roses. *We forgot that movie real quick!*

But remember, Shore is in the rink, and he doesn't want beer on the bus. So you have to think ahead. I have a plan. I start taking the tape off my pads before the game is over—I figure that will save me 30 seconds. Then, as the game ends, everyone is congratulating our goalie, Marcel Paille. I skate by, bang his pads and exit the ice. I get in the room, take off my gear and jump in the shower before the last guy is off the ice. I was so quick, I was showered, out the door with my bag, and leaving the building with the crowd!

I go across the street to this little place where you can get a couple of beers, and I get two six-packs. I quickly jump on the bus and put them underneath my seat before anyone has even gotten out of the dressing room.

Eddie sees me getting off the bus and says, "What's the hold-up? Get everyone on this bus!" He figured if I was ready, everybody should be. So I go back in the room and guys are still getting undressed. I'm laughing as I tell them, "Eddie wants to know what the hold-up is." Eddie comes in the room, and says, "Let's get moving!"

But as the guys start walking towards the bus, a few try to go across the street where I went to get some beer. Eddie yells, "Where you going? You're not going there, get on the bus now!" Luckily, we had the beer I bought tucked under my seat, coughing every time we opened one. It's a good thing, because Eddie had no intention of letting us have a good night out in Hershey.

Usually, we'd be there by 11 p.m. or so. But this time, we get on the highway, and Eddie says to our bus driver, Paul, "Slow this bus down!" Paul gets it down to 35, and Eddie says, "Slow it down more!" Paul says, "Mr. Shore, I'm doing 35 miles an hour on the Interstate with my flashers on." And Eddie say, "Who's paying you? Go slower!"

So, we drive all the way to Hershey doing 25! We don't get in till 2:00 in the morning! But we were determined. We had a pal there, Ummie, who had a bar we frequented. We call him when we arrive, and he's still there. He agrees to stay open for us if we come in the back door. A bunch of us go over and we're enjoying some food and drinks when there's a knock on the front door.

Ummie says, "I told you guys back door only!" He goes and opens it. It's Eddie Shore.

Now, he never said we couldn't go out, even though he tried to hijack our night, but he wanted to know who was there. He was keeping score. So Eddie sat at the bar by himself, having a couple of ryes.

Well, Pete Shearer was my roommate on this trip. Pete says, "I'm going to put some music on."

I say, "Don't, Pete! Eddie can't stand music!" But Pete didn't care. He walks right past Shore at the bar, puts his 50 cents in the jukebox for seven songs, which is what you got back then. Well, let's just say this wasn't nice music like Anne Murray, or Jerry Vale. Pete liked the songs that made lots of noise, and every song was louder than the last.

Eddie finished his drink, and walked out.

The next morning, the phone in our hotel room rings at 5:30 a.m. I answer, and it's Pat Egan, the coach. He wants to talk to Pete. So Pete grabs the phone, and talks for a minute, and then hangs up and gets out of bed.

I ask, "What's going on?"

"I gotta get dressed. I'm catching a 6:30 a.m. bus out of here for Springfield."

Eddie had sent him home.

And it was a horrible bus trip, too. Pete had to transfer in New York, or something ridiculous. We played that night, drove back to Springfield, and Pete only beat us home by a few hours. I told Pete that Eddie wouldn't like the music!

The funny thing is, they flew in a guy named Borden Smith for the game so we'd have a full roster. Well, Borden didn't play a shift. We lost, and Eddie was mad so he fined us all $100. Poor Borden flies in for one game, doesn't play, and it costs him a hundred bucks! At least Pete didn't have to pay the fine!

Act 3—Strike! The End of Eddie Shore

My last year in Springfield was also Eddie's last year.

We had won three straight Calder Cups, and Dale Rolfe, Bill White and David Amadio wanted raises. They were the three best defencemen in the league, as far as I was concerned. Of course, Eddie says, "No raise. You either take what I offer you or go home, because you can't play anywhere else." Which was true. He owned us.

So the three of them decided they weren't going to play unless they got an extra $500 each. A couple of days before the season, Eddie gave in, and they each got their $500.

But Eddie found a way to get it back. One night, early in the season, we lose 5-4 to the Quebec Aces. It was our last game before a week off. Eddie suspends all three guys for "indifferent play." That was what he suspended everyone for, no matter what the real reason.

The whole team was upset. We were at a Booster party the next night and the team came to me and asked if I would talk to Eddie. I wasn't the captain anymore, Jimmy Anderson was. He was a real good player, but a quiet guy, so the guys wanted me to speak for them. I said, "Okay, but not before I speak to every player to make sure that's what they want." One by one, they all said, "Yes." They wanted me to do it.

Bill White: *Killer was a great centreman, a senior guy on the team and he was respected by every man in that room. We knew he'd be the best spokesman for us.*

The next day, we show up at the rink and I tell the guys, "We're not going on the ice until I sort this out with Shore." He walks in, and I am waiting for him in the corridor. I say, "Mr. Shore, can I talk to you, please. I'm representing the players."

He says, "You represent fuck all!" And he walked in his office and slammed the door.

I walk back into the room and say, "Fellas, he says I don't represent fuck all. My advice is, we just get out." So we left. We were on strike, I guess.

This was Sunday. On Monday, we're having a players' meeting and the trainer walks in and says, "Killer, can I see you?" He pulls me aside and gives me a letter. I'm suspended for indifferent play. I scored a goal and had three assists, and was the star of the game in our last game, and I'm suspended for indifferent play!

It was a nerve-wracking week. I never really asked to get in the middle of this, but I was. I kept having meetings with the team twice a day, because I knew they were getting nervous.

Bill White: *I had two kids, and one on the way. I was scared. Things are going through your head, like "What am I going to do if he gets rid of us?" We were worried about our careers. We really didn't know which way it was going to go.*

I asked Gerry Foley to help me, because he was well respected by the other players. We stayed off the ice Monday and Tuesday, then Shore agreed to meet with me and Foley on Wednesday. "What are your demands?" Shore asked. We didn't really have demands. We just wanted proper medical care and proper equipment. Some of the equipment we used was left over from Eddie's playing days. It was falling apart. And we were never allowed a chisel to fix sticks the way we wanted.

We also wanted to be taken care of properly when we got injured. One time, I broke my jaw, and Shore made me run into the coach to see if I could handle the pain and still play. Often, he wouldn't let us go to the hospital. I broke my ribs once, and he wouldn't let me get X-rays. We went on a road trip to Quebec the next week, and I was in so much pain, I finally checked myself into hospital. They couldn't believe it when I told them I'd done it a week ago. Donny Johns once cut his Achilles tendon and needed surgery. He was supposed to stay in the hospital a while, but Eddie called and said, "If you don't get out of there now, you're suspended."

Finally, we wanted an end to those ridiculous "indifferent play" suspensions. But Eddie didn't give an inch. He told Gerry that all the players would be welcomed back, except for me. I'd be the only one suspended. But Gerry said, "No, we're in it together." So Shore kicked us out of the building.

The story was starting to appear in newspapers all over North America—"Hockey Team On Strike." Bill White said there was an agent named Alan Eagleson who might be able to help us. I recognized the name. He was Bobby Orr's agent. I don't think anyone else had an agent back then. So I called Eagleson and he says, "You've been making some headlines down there. You're in quite a pickle."

I said, "Yeah, we are. We didn't realize it would get like this and it's over my head now."

He said, "I'll be down there tonight."

We met in Hartford. Eagleson came down with another guy, Ray Smela. When Smela heard the stories about Eddie, he said, "My advice is to go home, and you'll all be free agents at the end of the year."

Eagleson had a meeting with Shore, but Eddie wasn't going to be bluffed by some agent. He just scoffed at him. So Eagleson told us we should go home.

Shore was already on the phone to the NHL, trying to get players. Toronto had three players down in Tulsa that got sent to Springfield, but they were the only ones. And once they showed up, they were on our side.

One night at home, the phone rings and Judy answers. She says, "Brian, he says its Clarence Campbell. He wants to talk to you." The president of the NHL was on the phone.

I get on the phone, and Campbell threatens me. He says, "Unless you get those players back, you will never play a game the rest of your life." And I say, "Well, Mr. Campbell, if Mr. Shore hadn't done all these things to us, we wouldn't be in this position." He hung up on me.

I called Eagleson right away. He called Campbell and told him if he didn't stay out of it, he'd go after the NHL's contract with its players, not just the AHL's. It worked. Besides those three players from Tulsa, there were no more threats.

We had a lot of support. Doug Harvey in Baltimore and Freddie Glover in Cleveland got their teams to hold sympathy strikes. They stopped in the middle of practice and sat down at centre ice in support of all the guys in Springfield.

We were winning. On the Saturday, Jack Butterfield, the president of the AHL, came to my house. He was related to Shore by marriage. We told him what we wanted: proper medical care, proper equipment and no more suspensions for "indifferent play."

So, Eagleson worked out a deal with them: the team comes back, we get our medical and equipment, and Eddie Shore can have nothing to do with the team for the rest of the year.

Later that day, on the radio, we hear that Eddie Shore is leaving the team for medical reasons and his son Teddy is taking over. The strike was over and our Saturday game was back on.

But they didn't want me to go to the game. Eddie's last request, I guess. The other three suspended defencemen weren't allowed to play, either. They didn't even want us in the building. But I said, "If I can't play, I'm going as a fan."

We walked into that building and the crowd went nuts. They had been for the players the whole time. We won the strike, and we annihilated Rochester, 8-2 or 9-2. Don Cherry was on that Rochester team, and he often says nobody would have beaten us that day. Eddie was gone and the reins were off.

Don Cherry: *Brian laid it on the line for those guys on his team. There were a few chickenshit guys who wanted to back out. But Brian wouldn't back down. You have to remember, Eddie Shore loved Brian like a son. He would have made him his coach someday, I know it. Brian risked everything to stand up for what he believed.*

That was the birth of the National League players' union. Our strike in Springfield started the whole thing. The union was in the National League by the next season. So was I. Nineteen sixty-seven was the year of expansion and I ended up with the LA Kings.

Of course, every team had to have a rep for the new players' association. A lot of guys were leery about being the rep, so they voted unanimously that I would do it. Our goalie, Terry Sawchuk, would be the assistant. Well, Terry was a super guy and I knew him from back in the Detroit days. He came up to me and said, "It's up to you, but I think you went through enough last year. I'm the number one pick (in the expansion draft). They can't do anything to me, but they sure might do something to you, so let me do it."

I said, "Deal. Thanks."

But I wasn't done with fighting for players' rights. A couple of years later, I was playing in Rochester with Don Cherry, and we were told there was going to be a meeting to try to start a players' association for the American League. Don told me no one was going, but I said, "Someone has to go. It could be really good for you guys."

So I went. And they talked about a new medical plan and a new dental plan, exactly what the guys needed. In fact, when our coach, Dick Gamble, heard about it, he asked if he could get in on it. I said, "Sure, it's for coaches as well as players."

The next day, I was notified I was being sent down to Tulsa, in the Central League. Then, Denny Morrison and Johnny Ingram were sent down from Baltimore to Seattle. The three of us, who were voted reps to the meeting, were all sent right out of the American League! We'd been blacklisted.

Oh, well, I don't regret it. I missed Rochester and I missed Don, but I believed in the benefits the union was going to get those players. So I went down to Tulsa, met some good young kids and had a great time.

I never look back. I've always believed everything happens for a reason, and things work out for the best.

Now, as for Eddie Shore, he was done after that season of the strike. The NHL expanded, he sold Springfield and retired.

He was a pain, but we did win three championships, and he did teach me a lot.

Eddie had some really different ideas about body position. The biggest key to hockey that most guys ignore is balance. Your thighs are the strongest muscle in your body. A lot of guys go into the corner and reach with their arms and stick, and get off balance. If you stay balanced over your thighs and don't reach, you have much better control. Eddie had a couple of drills about not getting your legs too wide apart, and keeping your body on top of your legs. I was always strong in the corners because I was on balance. Shore taught me that, and I used his drills in my coaching.

Also, he always focused on moving the puck. How quick can you move the puck? That's another thing we always worked on with the 67's.

I used quite a few of Eddie's drills my whole coaching career. But trust me, I never taped anyone's hands to his stick. Or put a noose around a goalie's neck.

7

Move the Puck! (And Killer's Other Hockey Commandments)

I have coached hockey the same way for 35 years. My philosophy has never changed. Remember at the beginning when I told you about smoking the same cigars and listening to the same Anne Murray tape? It's the same with the way I teach hockey. I stressed the exact same things every season—from the 1970s to when I left the bench in 2009.

1. Move the puck!
It drives me bananas when I see a forward or defenceman carrying the puck, his winger open eight feet in front of him, and he doesn't give him the puck! Now, the winger is stuck waiting, he's forced to slow down or he hits the line and he's

offside. Sometimes they will pass, but they wait too long, so when the forward does get the puck, he's lost his momentum and now he can't beat the defenceman. Move the puck quickly, instead of waiting that extra couple of seconds.

This is especially true for defencemen. I don't mind you being part of the play, I just don't want you to be the first man in the play. If the forward is ahead of you, give him the puck! Don't make him stop at the blue line, so the backcheckers catch up. Give it to him NOW.

Brad Shaw (Ottawa 67's defenceman, 1981–84): *When I first came to Ottawa, I always wanted to beat guys 1 on 1. I handled the puck way too much. So, one time, between periods, he says: "Shaw! Listen, there's a guy sitting up in Section 109 you haven't tried to beat yet. You've tried to beat everybody else, you might as well try him, too!"*

Killer knew I needed a kick in the rear end. And it worked. He stressed passing, and the importance of the stick-to-stick, tape-to-tape pass, more than anyone. I've been coaching for 10 years now and I try to have that same attention to detail that Killer stressed to me.

2. Pass outside the opposing player's stick.
By that, I mean that if you are coming down on a defenceman, don't get within three feet of him and then pass. He's got his stick out, ready to poke check you, so you pass outside his stick—outside his reach—then he will have no chance of intercepting it. So pass it early, then you can go

and get a return pass. Don't wait until you get inside his stick's reach.

3. Go to the net!

If you are a centreman, make the pass and then go to the net. Or, if you are going to be the high man, after you make your pass, stay facing the net so you will be looking at the guy you passed the puck to. Invariably, what happens is the centre will give the puck to the left winger and start following the winger, coming towards him and dropping behind. When you do that, you just made the defenceman's job easy because he doesn't have to go out of position to take you. He can take both guys at once. If I'm a right-handed shot and I follow my left winger, I've eliminated options. I can't believe how many players do this. They haven't been taught properly. They do it because it is open ice, the defenceman is backing up and so you have room. But when you do it, you've probably nullified a 3 on 2, and if you are a right-handed shot, you now have a nearly impossible angle to score. So keep it simple, go to the net, or stay facing the net. Don't make it easy on the defenceman.

Once you get to the net, stay in front of the net and face the puck!

How many times do we see guys skate 200 feet and end up behind the net? I always say to the guys, "How many goals did you score from behind the net last year?" "Uhh, well, Coach ... uhh ... none."

"So how many would you score if you stayed in front and got a rebound?" Lots!

Bruce Cline was the first guy who ever emphasized this when I joined Springfield. Bruce played with Bill Sweeney, and they were one of the highest scoring lines ever. Eddie Shore emphasized driving to the net and staying in front. We'd always do drills on it. And Bruce did it better than anyone. Bruce told me at the end of one season, "I got eight more goals this year by staying in front and picking up a rebound, than had I went behind the net." And he kept track religiously. I never forgot that. It became instinct with us. Shore would harp on it over and over. "Go to the net, stop, face the puck and look for the rebound." Simple. There are no rebounds behind the net.

4. If you're a defenceman, own the corners, and own the front of the net!

We learned this in Springfield from players like Don Cherry, Teddy Harris and Kent Douglas. They owned the corners. We won three Calder Cups in a row, and though we had some great scorers, the strength of those teams was the defence, and our goalie, Marcel Paille. Marcel was probably one of the best goalies I played with in my life. But his life was easier because our defence punished people in the corners and in front of the net. When you do that, you will win. Teddy Harris was 6-foot-2 or 6-foot-3 and all elbows and arms. Trust me, you didn't want to go into the corner

Baby Brian in the back yard, 1935.

Brian, about six years old,
in front of the Christmas
tree.

Brian, front left, with pals on Easter Sunday, 1943.

Ottawa East Outlaws, 1949. Brian is front row, left. His lifelong pal, Gary "Stump" Craig, is front row, third from right.

The wives of the Springfield players, enjoying a drink from the Calder Cup. Brian's wife, Judy, is third from the right and at far right is the inimitable Eddie Shore.

Brian as an LA King, 1967. He scored the first goal in the team's history.

Brian, in 1973, in a fur coat that Judy had given him. He was coaching the Ottawa South Canadiens midget team.

Brian in his first year as coach of the Ottawa 67's, 1974-75.

with Teddy. And Kent Douglas was just plain mean. Or take a look at the Broad Street Bullies. They were tough in those two places, and they dominated.

It is tougher with today's rules, but you can still own the front of the net if you use your body correctly and you don't come too high with your cross-check. You can still clear the net and you can still knock 'em down. It's about proper balance and toughness. Pretty soon, the forwards will be a lot less enthusiastic coming into your corner. So I tell all the young defencemen, "Finish your checks in the corners, and win the battles in front of the net for the rebounds. Do those two things and I guarantee you will be successful."

These are the things I have taught from day one. Some of my players come back a decade later from the NHL and say, "You're still using the same drills, eh?" Yes, I am. If they were successful for so many years, why would I change them?

Mark Edmundson (Ottawa 67's forward, 1992–95): *We had the same practice every day for two years. You knew at 4:03, you were doing this drill and 4:07, the next drill. You knew exactly what you were getting, and as long as you worked as hard as you could, he was a happy man. And we did, because he had this aura that made you not want to disappoint him.*

We do a lot of drills with the puck. Last time I checked, you couldn't score without it. All our drills have a lot of skating and a lot of puckhandling. I don't need pylons on the ice to mock-up this or that. Just skate and handle the puck.

When guys left the Ottawa 67's, they were good passers. I always tried to make sure of that. We stressed forehand and backhand passing so it became second nature to the guys.

I'd always say, pass it over an imaginary stick. Defenders always have their sticks out, poking. So make saucer passes, just three or four inches off the ice, and make the puck land flat. Lead the guy, and make sure the pass lands flat. We'd work on it over and over and over. I don't care if you put it 30 feet in front of him, he can always speed up and get it. Just put it over the imaginary stick.

And I worked a lot on shooting, too. There's a knack to shooting. I never had a great shot, but I'd always stress to the players to use wrist shots more. Don't make everything a slap shot. So many guys these days always try to slap the puck. The wrist shot is quicker and very dangerous. You can catch the goalies more off-guard.

One of the greatest satisfactions in coaching is watching a player improve. I don't think any player I had improved more than Adam Creighton. His skating wasn't very good when he arrived, but, boy, did he come a long way.

I think I helped Bobby Smith, too. When he arrived, he was more of a one-dimensional player. He would try to stick-handle, and beat his guy, and he'd end up on his backhand, which is a much tougher shot. Bobby learned to pass the puck, forehand and backhand. He had Steve Payne on his right and Timmy Higgins on his left. Steve had 57 goals. Bobby set up an awful lot of them. He was always destined for stardom—I can't take credit for that—but I think I helped him understand the importance of his wingers.

Jim Fox (Ottawa 67's forward, 1977–80): *I vividly remember sitting on our bench in Ottawa, and Bobby gets the puck right in front of me at our blue line, and on his backhand, he throws an NFL pass, across the ice, blue line to blue line, and it lands right on Steve Payne's stick in full flight. And just like that, Payne was on a breakaway. I just sat there and said, "Holy shit." Bobby Smith could make the puck talk.*

You certainly can't take credit for guys like Jimmy Fox. He came to Ottawa with the hands and head of a pro. It was the same for Dougie Wilson. I'd like to say I really helped Dougie Wilson, but he could shoot, skate and pass through the eye of a needle.

My goals for the players I coached were simple. I wanted them to become better players, and by skating every day and handling the puck every day, that was going to happen.

I'd always tell them, "You are going to become a good hockey player here. Whether you can become an NHLer, I don't know that. But I do know that hockey can give you a living, and can help you become a better person no matter what you do with your life. Someday, you are going to have to get a job, and so while you are here, you may as well learn the other important things—manners, respect, honesty, accountability, being a team-first individual. We can help you with all of those things."

Alyn McCauley (Ottawa 67's forward, 1993–97): *Account-ability to your teammates, to yourself, was one thing he really taught me about. And leadership. Before my third year, he called me into his office. He said he was going to make me captain, but he had certain expectations. He wanted me to be around my teammates more, to hang out with them. It was something I hadn't done enough of before. That was a big part of leadership to him. Good team chemistry off the ice will be beneficial on it. That lesson made a huge difference in my NHL career. I'm a scout now with the LA Kings, and we focus on it.*

All our players dream of making the National League. But I'd stress to them that making a life in hockey might mean the National League; it might mean the American League, or the Eastern League; it might mean Europe. But you can make a living at it and it's a great life. Make no mistake, hockey isn't work.

And sometimes that door to the hockey world won't open. It's not only ability; a lot of it is timing. So, I tried to teach them things that would help them step into the working world.

I'd tell them, "It's important to get your education while you are with us. Maintain your grades and good conduct so if hockey doesn't work out, you're ready to go to university when your junior playing days are over. It's a great program they have now where the years you spend in junior hockey help pay for your schooling.

"And your hockey career isn't over when you go to university. Especially now, the universities are supplying hockey players to the pros. So, junior can give you a ticket to university, and you can get an education and still chase your dream."

I tried to teach them how to be good hockey players, but also teach them things that would help them even if they didn't end up in hockey.

It wasn't just about moving the puck. (But they had better move that puck.)

8

Ralph

JD: *As you've already read, there are countless characters who have skated through Killer's life. But there is no one who gets the coach laughing harder than Jim Ralph. Ralph played goal (and team comedian) for Killer for four seasons in Ottawa (1979–83). He's one of the two goalies on Killer's All-Time 67's team, along with Darren Pang. Ralph was drafted by the Chicago Black-hawks, but a serious knee injury put a halt to his NHL dreams, and he never made it beyond the minors. He is now the radio analyst for the Toronto Maple Leafs, and still one of the funniest men in hockey. (If you ever have a chance to hear him speak, at a golf tournament or banquet, don't miss it.) Killer has so many stories involving Ralph, and vice versa, I figured the only way to sort out the truth was to get them together. The pair has kept in touch, but they hadn't seen each other for a couple of years when we sat down for a couple of pops one night in Toronto. This is a transcript of that conversation:*

Ralph: So where's the cigar?

Killer: I brought only about eight down. I have to spread them out. Good to see you, Ralph. Hey, you know who is back in the Soo? Seamus Kotyk.

JD: *Kotyk, like Ralph, is a former Ottawa 67's goalie from Sault Ste. Marie, Ontario.*

Ralph: Hey, that reminds me, you have to change your team website. You still have him as being the winningest goalie in franchise history.

Killer: He isn't? You are?

Ralph: Geez, Coach, he has 70-something. I was 108!

Killer: Well, I better change that as soon as I get back. I'll tell them Ralph has threatened never to mention the 67's on the radio again. (*Sarcastically*) That'll terrify them.

JD: So, were you the one who wanted to draft Ralphie?

Killer: Yup. First pick. I said to our scouts, "We have some good forwards; we have enough good defencemen; we have to get a goalie we can use for four years." I didn't want to be looking for a goalie every year. I wanted a 16-year-old to come in one year to learn and then look after us for the next three years. So, I took Ralph with the first pick. But you know what happened? I was really happy we got him, so I drove all the way to the Soo. I get there, and his Dad says they can't see me that day because they have to go meet with an agent who wants to give Ralph some highfalutin' demands.

Ralph: We didn't know anything! We were told all the Gretzkys and Coffeys, they were getting their palms greased to sign with the junior teams. This agent, Frank Caputo, contacted us. He had some guys like Greg Millen and Ronnie Francis, so we figured he knew what was going on. I was 16, and my Dad was new at this, too. We had no idea what we were doing. Frank said, "We'll get you $500 a month and a car." It sounded good to me. Anyway, we said, "Well, if that's the way it works, we're in." But then we made the mistake of calling Sam Pollock here. No wait, I think Killer called us, and ... well ... tell him what you said to Frank.

Killer: I said, "Fine. Tell Ralph to stay home. You can look after him and pay him that much money to stay in Sault Ste. Marie." Then I hung up.

Ralph: Actually, I think it was more like, "He gets what everybody else gets or you can tell him to f-off and stay home!" (*Laughter*) (*Ralph does a dead-on Killer impersonation.*)

So, Frank comes back and says, "Well, Brian was a little upset but everything will be okay." And we're like, "What the fu ... a little upset? You told us this was the way it was supposed to be done!?!" So we call back and try to calm things down. Killer say he will call back Friday night and we'll talk about it more. This was the week before training camp. So, Friday night comes and it's six o'clock. Then seven o'clock. Then eight o'clock. No call. And I'm thinking, "He doesn't want me anymore! He's that mad. I'm done! First goalie ever to get drafted as an underage in the first round, and it's over for me already!" Now, 11:00 or 11:30 p.m., the phone finally rings and it's Eddie Hospodar, one of Killer's players. He says, "Brian apologizes, he just had emergency knee surgery." He had come out of the surgery and remembered he was supposed to call me. That made us feel a little better.

Killer: I blew out my knee and had to get it done right away so I'd be ready for training camp. First thing I said when I woke up after the surgery. "Call Jimmie Ralph for me."

I wanted him in Ottawa. I just had to talk some sense into him about that agent.

Ralph: So, Eddie Hospodar says, "Brian hopes to see you at camp." And that was it. We told the agent, "We're going." No more demands by us!

Killer: Good move. I never paid anything extra to a first-rounder. Ever.

Ralph: Well, you better not have after you put me through that. Jesus.

Killer: I've had other players, first-rounders, saying, "We want this and we want that." And I always said, "Not in Ottawa you don't." I could never walk into a room and tell the guys, "Everyone is getting the same," knowing a couple of guys are getting more. I just couldn't do it. And it's the same today. No Ottawa 67's player is getting a special deal.

JD: What did players get paid back then?

Ralph: If you had a car, you got $55 a week. I think it was $25 for everyone else.

Killer: The school plan was $25 a week. You would still get paid for the weeks you went home, in March, and the spring when the season was over.

Ralph: But I never went home, I moved in with you!

JD: Did you live with Killer your first year in Ottawa?

Killer: No, he moved in with a family, and he told me after a few weeks, "Every day all I'm eating is Kraft Dinner." And I said, "Kraft Dinner? What's wrong with that? I love Kraft Dinner! Quit complaining!"

Ralph: I think I moved in with you because my billet family was moving. Not sure why, but it seemed every year my billet family moved. *(Laughter)* Anyway, I think it was just after my third year, right around when I signed with Chicago that I moved in with you. It was only for three months, but there are about 300 stories. Billy, Killer's son, was about my age. We got really close. I still call him "Brother Bill," and I still call Judy "Mom." Judy ran the ship. She had a rewards system. "Jimmy, you cut the grass then you can have a beer."

Killer: Or cut the mat. Ralph ran right over the guest mat with the lawn mower. Shredded it.

Ralph: True. But here's the thing. He's sitting on the back porch, always listening to the Expos game on the radio. Never watching it on TV, always on the back porch on the radio.

So, he says to me, "Ralph! What are you doin' today, Ralph?" I say, "Well, I was going to ..." "Well, good, you can cut the f'in' grass first, Ralph." So I cut the grass and I run over the mat at the side door. So Judy comes home and she doesn't notice the mat. She says, "Jimmy, how good a husband is Brian? I ask him to cut the grass this morning, and I come home and the grass is cut." I say, "Hey, I cut the grass!"

The best was, Killer always makes breakfast on Sunday mornings. That's the family tradition. So, the first weekend I was there, I had this room in the basement, and I think I might have gone out the Saturday night."

Killer *(Sarcastically)*: Ya think?

Ralph: It's a safe bet. So, it's morning and he's banging on my bedroom door. "Ralph! Get up, you're having breakfast, Ralph. You're not sleeping all day, Ralph!" So I put a robe on and I stagger upstairs and I sit at the table and he says, "Ralph, come here." So, he brings me into the kitchen and says, "Ralph, you're sitting in a f'in' robe at my table with my daughter sitting there, and that thing of yours is swinging back and forth underneath! Go get some clothes on!" So, I go downstairs, but instead of getting dressed, I just put another robe on, and come back up. "Ralph!!!!" *(Laughter)*

JD (Awkward aside for readers): *Jim Ralph is somewhat famous in hockey circles for being ... umm ... how do I put this? Physically ... gifted.*

Killer: What about that one evening meal? I always had my special chair at the end of the table. It was the only one with arms. The other chairs had no arms. I'm always at the end of the table. ALWAYS. So, one night, Judy says, "Oh, Jimmy, tonight you sit here." So, he gets the armchair, and then she comes out with a plate for him with half the roast on it. "Here, Jimmy, you must be hungry." So he's got the big thick cut of roast beef. Then she brings me mine, and it looked like the scraps, a couple of stringy little pieces! So I say, "Hold it! We have a problem here. I own the house. I'm the one buying the food! He's in my seat! He's got my plate! And he's got my roast! These scraps are his!"

Ralph: He didn't let that happen again. Here's another one. At the end of my last season, Killer's son Billy and I decide to take a trip to Florida. It was Earl Montagano, one of the 67's owners, whose daughter had the travel agency. We booked it all through her. We were going to stay at the Yankee Clipper in Fort Lauderdale. We got the airline tickets and everything else we needed, and we thought we had paid for everything. But it turns out we paid only for the airfare. So, we go down to Florida, and we're having a great time. Then, three days later, we get a call from the front desk saying, "You have to settle up." Settle up? We thought we already paid at the travel agency. So, now we're screwed. We're running out of money. We were desperate. We went to this place called Durty Nellys, where you got a free hot dog during happy hour. That was dinner. And here's a funny side story. We're sitting at Durty Nellie's, and Billy's talking about all his Dad's favorite players. He starts talking about Dougie Wilson, and I look down the bar and see this guy, and say, "Hey, that guy kinda looks like Dougie Wilson. Hey, it is Dougie Wilson!" Billy must have said his name two minutes before! Dougie was getting married, and he was down with his buddy for one last trip before the wedding. So Dougie says, "We're going to a place called The Cheetah, you want to come?" We said, "No, we'll just hang here." Dougie looks at us and says, "You don't have any money, do you?" So, Dougie helped us out. We rode his wallet for one day, but we couldn't do it any longer. So, we had to call home and ask a certain someone to wire us money."

JD: How did that go over?

Ralph: What do you think? I'll tell you how stupid I am. Billy had already called and he got a blast of shit from Killer. So, the phone rings in the hotel room and Billy says, "You get it." Stupid me, I do. It's Killer. "Ralph! I can't afford to go on a f'in' trip, but you two idiots, apparently, I can send you on one. How f'in' stupid can you be?!?"

Killer: I had already sent the money. But they were going to hear about it.

JD: Were you really mad?

Killer: I made them think I was.

Ralph: Here's the best part. We wanted to save enough money to make sure we could bring back a case of Bud, because that was the only American beer Killer drank. We thought that would be our great peace offering. We get back in Ottawa and they meet us at the airport. Judy says, "It's so great you're home. The house was so quiet without you, you look so tanned . . ." She was her usual sweet self. And Killer is just standing there in the airport, puffing on a cigar. Just staring at us. We say, "Killer, we brought you a case of Budweiser." Not a word. Not a smile. Nothing. Billy looks at me and whispers, "Uh oh. We're still in trouble." So the whole way home Judy is talking, asking us, "How was it? What did you do?" We're in the back seat of the car and Killer is looking back at us in the rear-view mirror, but not saying a word. He's just puffing on that cigar. Finally, he stops at a light and says, "Hey, Ralph, Billy. I was thinking. If I save up real hard, how would you like to go to f'in' Hawaii next year?!?" *(Laughter)*

Killer: You should have seen Judy's face. I was trying hard not to laugh.

Ralph: So, I owed him about $600.

Killer: He paid me back in nickels.

Ralph: Pretty much. Actually, at the hockey school the next year, I brought him the money and he says, "Ralph, give me $100 and next time pay for your own trip." He wouldn't take all the money back. That's the kind of guy he really was.

JD: So, that's Killer, the landlord. What about Killer, the coach?

Ralph: He was tough, but I loved it. One time, we played in Peterborough on Saturday, and then we played in Maple Leaf Gardens Sunday afternoon. Larry Floyd hit me with about three minutes left up in Peterborough. Now remember, the equipment was different back then. He got me up in the collarbone part of the muscle. I could barely lift my arm. The next morning, we're on the bus, and Taff (the trainer) comes back and says, "Killer wants to know if you're okay." I say, "Well, I can't lift my arm." He goes up to the front of the bus, comes back and says, "Killer says you're okay." So I guess I'm playing! I put the heat rub on it, and the trainer helps me get dressed because I can't move my arm. But as we go through warm-up, it starts to loosen up. We end up winning, 2-1.

Killer: He had a shutout going into the last minute. He'd already been chosen first star of the game, and they tie it up with about 40 seconds left. It breaks the shutout and ties the game. Am I right?

Ralph: Yup. We won it in overtime.

Killer: No, we scored in the last few seconds of regulation. Were you just testing my memory there?

Ralph: Oh, right. As long as you remembered I was first star, I didn't care about the rest. (Laughter)

So we get into the dressing room, I'm feeling pretty good about my game when Killer comes in. He's saying this and that and then he goes, "And Ralph, the next time you say you're hurt, you'll play 60 games in a row, ya dumb-ass!" Just screaming at me! And I never missed another game the rest of my hockey career until my knee injury.

Killer: You should have had me that year.

Ralph: Yeah, you would have said, "Just tape it, Ralph!"

Oh, here's another one. We used to have pre-season games against Hull that were just brawls. One scrap after another. One night, we're playing in Hull and their guy slashes me. So I slash him back, and he turns and drops his gloves. Then one of our defencemen turns around, slides on his knees, and grabs him around his waist. Now the guy can't move. So I start whaling away. There's blood everywhere, and I'm feeling pretty good. Even though I have my mask on, and my teammate is holding the guy as I pound him, I'm feeling proud. Killer comes in to the room after and says, "Ralph! What's the matter with you, you stupid prick! You could have broken your hand!" I went from sky-high to wanting to hide.

Hey, Killer, we have to tell him the famous story, right?

Killer: I told him he can't put that one in the book.

JD: I'll let Ralph tell it. Then you can blame him.

Ralph: Okay. Well, it was a cardinal sin to lose on a Friday night at home. There were always 8,000 to 10,000 people in the rink. You just couldn't lose at home on Friday. So, Peterborough was up on us 3-0 after the first, and the third goal was really ugly. He fired it from about centre.

I tried to put one knee down and put my stick in front of my pad, but I knocked the stick and flipped it forward, and the puck went off my stick. Now I'm handcuffed, and the puck just trickles across the line.

Killer: I say he looked down like he thought he had it, and then he looked over at the bench and the crowd was going "Oooooooh!" And he was just looking at me, because ...

Ralph: I knew I was going to get it. So, we're in the dressing room after the period, and Killer comes in. He would always stand at 10 and 2, you know with one foot at 10 and the other at 2. So, if you were at 12, you knew you were getting it. So he starts at one side of the room, and he's going through everybody, and I know he's going to get me last. Finally, he gets to me. He says, "Ralph, that shot! You could have stopped it with your cock!" And he walks out!

Killer: Well, he could have. That thing is a curling rock. So then I poke my head back in the room, and say, "And by the way, I wish I had it!" And I walked out. Well, the whole room just cracked up.

Ralph: Then we go out and win 8-5 or something. You know that stupid question reporters always ask, "What was said in the first intermission?" Imagine if someone asked it. "Well, the coach said I could have stopped it with my unit."

Killer: We never used those big motivational speeches. I just said whatever came to my mind. If I made them laugh, it usually loosened them up.

Ralph: Killer always said, "If I'm pissed off, I'll tell you, and then it's over. If you carry a grudge, it's your grudge, because to me, it's forgotten the next day." He would give it to you hard, but then it would be over. And if you came in the next day pouting, he'd give it to you again for pouting.

JD: How long did it take you to learn this, because it must be intimidating when you're 16 years old?

Ralph: Yes, but the first year, he protected me.

Killer: The 16-year-olds, I don't get the first year. I make sure no one picks on them.

Ralph: The second year was harder, and then the last two years he pushed me as hard as he could. And it worked.

JD: Ralphie's too modest to say it, but he was about the funniest guy you ever coached, wasn't he?

Killer: He was. Ralph and Sean Simpson. Wouldn't matter, win, lose or draw, we'd get on the bus after a game, and within five minutes, they'd say, "Can we have the mic?" The two of them would entertain the whole way home. Pretty soon you'd forget whether you won or lost. Ralph would do Danny Gallivan and Foster Hewitt. Simmer would do these skits. They should have had their own TV show.

JD: When did you start all these imitations?

Ralph: In high school, but I never thought I'd have an audience for it.

JD: Did you impersonate Killer when you played for him?

Ralph: All the time, but only behind his back.

JD: Did you do imitations of any players?

Ralph: John Linseman. Ken's brother. He had this slow drawl. Sim and I both did him. One time, Killer was taking us to the Montreal Forum for a game. He says, "Don't wear any of those bum jeans you guys wear. You're representing the Ottawa 67's, you wear a suit." So, we're in the office and Sean Simpson runs around to the secretary's desk and calls Killer. So we're standing at Killer's door, but we can also see Sim on the phone. So Sim says, "Heyyyy, Killerrrr, John Linsemannnnn." Killer says, "Hey, John, what do you want?" Sim says, "I was ... just ... wonderinnnn' ... if I wore. ... newwww jeans ... that weren't ... rrrripped, if that was ... okayyyy?" Killer goes, "No, John! I said No f'in' jeans on the trip, John!" "Welllllll ... what if I wearrrr a long ... coooooat ... over the jeaaaans?" Killer is so mad at this point, it was hilarious.

Killer: Then I caught on. So I sneak out of my office while he's still doing the impersonation. Now I'm standing over him at her desk, and he's doing his routine. So I say, "Sim, why don't you talk to me." He looks around and says, "Oh. Hi, Coach."

I didn't give him trouble. It was too funny.

That John Linseman was somethin'. We're going on a three-day road trip and he gets on the bus and he has nothing but his coat. So I say, "John, we're going on a road trip, where's your bag?" He says, "Where are weeee goinnnn'?"

I say, "We're going away for three games!" He says, "I brought my toooooothbrush." That was it. He brought his toothbrush for a three-game trip! Didn't even bring toothpaste. He bummed that off the other guys.

JD: Ralphie, you liked to have fun. Did he ever have to give it to you for missing curfew?

Ralph: I'll tell you one I missed. We lost at home on a Friday and Killer says, "Get on the f'in' bench, you pricks, and stay there!" And he went off and came back with a jacket and a whistle and skates. Some of the crowd is still there and they're going, "What is going on?" Killer has his windbreaker over his suit, with his whistle around his neck, and he says, "Ralph, get off the ice!"

Killer: Ralph was playing unbelievable. That game was against the Toronto Marlies. We had a two- or three-goal lead at the end of the second period. But I didn't like what I saw. I told them at the end of the second period, "You guys are letting them take it to you, and you are going to lose this game. The only one playing out there is Ralph." So, we go out, they tie the game up, and we lose. And I had told them, "If we lose this game, stay on the ice, don't bother getting off." So I made them skate hard. But I made Ralph leave. I usually don't do things that split a team, but I just couldn't make him skate. He'd made 40 or 50 saves.

Ralph: But you still yelled at me because I didn't want to go! I wanted to take it like everybody else. Anyway, I went to my girlfriend's, and Killer was so mad, he called everyone for curfew. I missed it. Sorry.

Killer: I hate curfews. For me to call one, I had to be really upset.

JD: You had good teams when Ralphie was there, but you never won a Memorial Cup?

Killer: No, but Ralph won one, with Kitchener.

Ralph: Yup. Those were the days when teams could still pick a goalie up from someone in their league. Kitchener beat us out in the league final in '82. That was Bellows, Al MacInnis, Scotty Stevens. They were good, but I didn't want to go. They had just beat us out. Why do I want to go play for the team that beat us? I also remembered when Killer picked up Patty Riggin for the Memorial Cup a couple of years before. Riggin gave up a horseshit goal on a backhand in the final, and they lost. All that anyone talked about was how Patty Riggin, who played his whole career in London, screwed Ottawa in the Memorial Cup. I thought, "I don't want to do that." Joe Crozier was the coach in Kitchener, and he asked me to come with them. I said, "Sorry, Joe, I'm not interested." Well, the next morning the phone rings, it's you-know-who. "Ralph! You stupid prick! You have a flight to Toronto at 10:00. You're going to Kitchener, and you're going to play with them in the Memorial Cup!" Now, at this point, I didn't really have to listen to Killer, because my junior career was done. But I listened.

Killer: He won them the Cup. They had lost a game, and with one more loss they would have been eliminated.

Ralph goes in and stones them. Then they went back to their own guy.

Ralph: Joe Crozier said to me before the last game against Sherbrooke, "If Wendel Young gives up a goal in the first five minutes, you're going in." Well, you've never seen anybody cheer harder in their life. Mike Vernon and I had been out every night late, hammered. Vernon got picked up by Portland, same deal as me, so we were both hoping if we got caught out, they wouldn't play us! It just wasn't the same as being there with your own team.

Killer: Ralph was a really good goalie, and he was an easy guy to coach because he never thought he was the star. He never got big-headed. He made fun of himself more than anyone else. He never blamed anyone for making a mistake or costing him a shutout. Everybody liked him. His last year was 1982–83, and then Darren Pang came in and won the Memorial Cup. I thought Ralph was destined for the National League. I think when he went to Chicago, they had Tony Esposito and another guy, and it was tough to crack. It was a dead end.

Ralph: I was drafted after my second year in junior by Chicago in the eighth round. Then the next two years in junior I made the All-Star team, but that was the way it was, everybody got drafted on spec. A few years into my pro career, Tony Esposito retired. So Murray Bannerman was going to be the starter, and ... Do you remember a goalie named Warren Skorodenski? Me and Skoro were battling to see who is going to be the backup goalie for the Black-hawks. Camp comes, Skoro starts great and I'm horseshit. Then I get better, and he gets worse. So, we get called in to see Pullie (Chicago GM Bob Pulford). Now, usually when Pullie wants to see you, you're gone! But we figure he can't get rid of both of us. So Pullie goes, "We had three guys who said you were better, Ralph; the other three said Skoro was better." So, here was the deal Pullie came up with: Skoro was married and I wasn't, so I was being sent down to the minors until Christmas. Skoro would get to stay with his wife in Chicago, then we'd switch. Whoever they decided was better in their stint would stay in Chicago for good. Pullie says, "The team plays January 1 in Boston. You're switching January 2."

Skoro didn't play a lot, maybe six or seven starts, but enough for them to have a look. So it's December 26, Toledo, Ohio. I go down on my left knee, I had my right leg out. Rene Badeau and Chris McSorley, Marty's brother, are behind me. Badeau pushes him and they both fall on me. My ACL was gone, my MCL was rolled up. I was done.

Here's the great part of the story. Three weeks later, Bannerman got hurt, and Skorodenski got hurt! So they called up my backup from Milwaukee. And Darren Pang played his first NHL game. The little prick! I think Panger's seventh or eighth pro game was in Chicago. Funny how hockey works.

Killer: You know, I always believe things work out for the best. You may think it was a setback because you didn't have a more successful pro career. But if you had, who is to say you would have been able to have the career you have now, and all the fun you have entertaining people.

Ralph: No regrets. I'll say this though. Along with all the fun and great stories, the line from Killer that I'll never forget was, "There are two things I can't stand: a liar and a thief. And a liar is worse." So then you go to pro hockey and ... well ... there are too many liars. And I couldn't stand it. If someone was lying to me, the gloves were off. Because to me, Killer's word was worth more than 300 signed legal documents. And that's the most important lesson he taught me: to be a man of my word—that integrity and honesty come before everything else. I also learned the world doesn't always work that way.

Killer: But you can make *your* world work that way.

Ralph: Yes, but I would get in these scraps with coaches and stuff in my pro career, because they weren't like you. There's no one like Killer.

JD: You're on his All-Time 67's team. Did you know that?

Ralph: That's a given. (*Laughter*) I had to speak at some event after you set that record for most coaching wins. Seven hundred and ... what was it?

Killer: 742. It passed Ken Hodge out in Portland.

Ralph: Right. And so I said in my speech, "I just have one thing to say. You're welcome." *(Laughter)*

I often tell people I helped put you in the Hall of Fame. Unfortunately, I put a lot more forwards in the Hall of Fame. *(Laughter)*

JD: *We turned off the tape recorder at that point. The laughs continued deep into the night.*

9

Grapes and Me

Don Cherry and I survived Eddie Shore together. That will bond you for life. It did. He is still one of my best friends.

Don is famous for those wild suits, but people don't realize he was always an immaculate dresser, even as a young player. He didn't wear the colorful stuff he wears today, but his shoes shined perfectly, his suit would be pressed perfectly. He was the neatest guy I knew.

And it wasn't just clothes.

Back when we were playing in Rochester in the American League, Don had this car that he kept absolutely spotless. It was always shined, always perfect.

Don would come by and pick me up to go to the rink, and my wife Judy would go pick up Don's wife Rose. We each had only one car, so that's the way it always worked.

Well, I liked my cigars, even back then. So, Don comes to pick me up one day, and I have my cigar going, and he locks the doors. I'm standing there outside in the cold and he says, "They're going to stay locked until you throw that cigar away."

That was Don and his car. The ashtrays were never used, the floors looked like no one had ever stepped on them, the seats looked like they were just shampooed, there wasn't a speck of dust on the dashboard. It looked like he drove it out of the showroom.

One day, Don says, "This car is getting old, I'm going to have to get rid of it. I don't want anyone else to have it. They would abuse it by driving too fast. They'd smoke in it, and get it dirty . . . it's not right. So after practice, come with me. We're going to burn it."

That's right. Don wanted to burn his car, so no one else could ever misbehave with it.

But while talking with the guys, I heard that one of our teammates, Lynn Zimmerman, was looking for a car. Lynn was one of our goalies. I said to Don, "Zimmerman is looking for a car. He doesn't have much money, so he might be interested if you're going to get rid of it."

Well, Don was a nice guy, so he says to Lynn, "You want my car?"

Lynn says, "Sure, Don, but how much you want for it?"

"I don't want nothing for it. But listen, I don't allow smoking in my car."

Lynn says, "I don't smoke, Don."

"No dirt is allowed on my car, inside or out."

"Sure, Don, I'll keep it clean."

"And when I come to the rink, I'm going to check to make sure it's clean, and if it's not, I'm taking it back!"

So, Don gave the car to Lynn. And it was a good car, because Don had taken care of it. I remember him telling me years later, "I should have kept that car."

One night a few weeks later, we were coming down to the rink and I was driving, and Don says, "Hold on a minute. I see my car over there." So, he walks over and circles around it and does a complete inspection.

He walks into the dressing room and says, "Lynn, good job. The car looks good." He just wanted him to know he was checking.

Don Cherry: *Battleship Kelly wanted the car, too. It came down to Zimmy and Battleship. It was a 1964 Pontiac Parisienne, burgundy with black upholstery. I was ready to burn it, too. Was on my way to this fella's farm. I wanted that car to go out like a Viking. But I gave it to Zimmy. And he kept it for 30 years!*

I told you before how Don invented the way to keep beer cold on the bus, by hanging it out the window in a pillowcase.

He still calls it his greatest contribution to hockey. We had fun on those bus trips. We never liked to eat a full meal. We just had cheese and crackers, and beer. We took turns. One day, I'd bring the cheese and crackers, and he'd bring the beer. Then we'd switch. You weren't allowed beer on the bus. Shore's rules. So we'd have to sneak them on, and cough real loud when we opened them.

Shore was tough on Don. One night on the road, we went out and some came back earlier than others. Let's just say Don and I were among the "others." Our coach, Pat Egan, saw him come in late and called Shore. So, he fined Don playoff money. A bunch of us were out, but Don was the one they were looking to catch.

Don took it all. Boy, was he tough. We were black aces one day. Those were the guys who weren't going to dress for the game, so they skated long after all the other players had left to rest up for the game. It was Don and me, Orland Kurtenbach, a big tough kid from the west, and our coach, Pat Egan. There isn't much to do for one or two hours on the ice when you're a black ace, so we had a game: Don and me against Kurtenbach and Egan.

Don is rushing down the ice near the boards and Egan cross-checks him. And I mean a hefty cross-check. Don gets mad. Real mad. Egan isn't wearing shoulder pads, and a few minutes later, he tries to cut around Don, and Don just crunches him with the stick. I think he broke the stick he hit him so hard. This is our coach!

"Two can play at that game," Don says to Egan.

Don Cherry: *Pat Egan really hated me. Even more than Shore did. I knew he was trying to hurt me. So I got him good. He was a tough Irish guy, so he wouldn't let on he was hurt. But he was hurt bad. The next day, I got a letter I was being sent down to Three-Rivers.*

Eddie says to him, "You're going to Three-Rivers in the Quebec League." Don says, "How do you get there?" Shore answers, "You get to the border and turn left."

JD: *That is one of the scenes recreated in the 2010 movie about Don Cherry.*

Don was fuming. But he went to Three-Rivers. He had some tough times. It was a real French community. But he persevered, and he helped that team. Like I said, Don was a survivor.

Don would do anything to win. He was a sixth defenceman, but he was always a great teammate. I think he liked me because I was as competitive as he was. Even when we went on the road, my game didn't change. I always played hard, even though I wasn't one of the best players on the team. Don appreciated that.

We had a couple of good arguments because I would stick up for Shore sometimes, but we became the best of friends, and stayed that way after our playing days were over.

Even though he's probably the most famous guy in Canada, there are some things people don't know about Don. Like how much he loves drums. Back in Rochester, he used to play the drums, and I'd come over and watch him. One time, he came down to watch the Changing of the Guard in Ottawa. Don, his wife Rose, my wife Judy and I went down to watch it. But watching wasn't enough for him. Don joined them! He just fell into line right on Wellington Street in front of the Peace Tower. He marched with the band all the way down Elgin Street to Laurier to the Drill Hall! He loved it.

But not as much as he loved his dog, Blue.

I remember the first time I met Blue. This is the first Blue, the original. We were retired, and Don had a hockey school in Rochester. He asked me to come down to help out because he was going off to coach Team Canada.

They were getting me a little flat to stay in, but the first night I stayed with Don and Rose, in their basement. Don had this beautiful big aquarium. That's another thing people don't know about him: he loves fish. He wouldn't look at the TV, he'd just watch the fish. He'd point to each one and tell me what type it was.

And he adored Blue. He got him to be a protection dog for Rose and his kids, Cindy and Tim. He was a tough-looking dog—huge neck—not a good-looking dog. I told Don that. He says, "Blue, you hear that? Killer's talking about you. He says you're not good-looking."

Anyway, I go to sleep downstairs. All of a sudden, in the middle of the night, I wake up, and Blue's head is on my arm and his face is about an inch away from mine and he's just staring at me.

"Hi, Blue."

There's no way I am going to move and disturb this scary-looking beast in the middle of the night, so I didn't budge. I stayed in the exact same position all night out of sheer fear. I suppose he liked me, but I wasn't taking any chances.

Don Cherry: *See. I told you Brian was sharp.*

In the morning, I heard Rose come down to make some coffee, so I called her downstairs to have a look at me and my bedmate. Rose laughs and says, "Don't move, Brian. Don! Come see where your beloved dog is."

I hear Don saying, "Where's my Blue?" He walks in and has a look at his dog lying with me, and says, "Bad boy, Blue, you're supposed to sleep with me!" We had a good laugh. But I still wasn't budging until Blue did.

Don trusted me, and it's a good thing. The first day I was at his hockey school while he was away with Hockey Canada, a couple of the guys he'd hired to teach the kids showed up late for their session. They were players on the Rochester team he was coaching. They came out to the ice late, and then sat on the bench and had a coffee. The kids and I were already out on the ice. I went to them and said, "You guys are Don's instructors?"

"Yes."

"Well, I'll take your shifts for the rest of the week if you can't show up on time."

I fired them both.

Don calls me later and says, "How'd it go at the school?" I said, "Well, I fired two of your instructors. If they can't show up on time and be ready and be attentive to those kids, they're no use to me."

Don said, "Good." I was a little leery about firing his guys, but he felt the same way I did about that kind of stuff. When we were with Shore, if you weren't on the ice five minutes early, you were late. So Don agreed. He always supported me, even if I got him in trouble, which I sometimes did.

We always coach the CHL Top Prospects Game together. One year, Lanny McDonald was our honorary coach. Don kept telling the kids, "Make sure you come up the boards with the puck." Well, the game is tied early in the third period, and one of our guys tries to come right through the slot in his own end. Bing-bang-bong! They score, and we're down. Exactly what Don had told them NOT to do.

Lanny comes to me and says, "What do you want me to do?"

I say, "Bench him."

Remember this is a Prospects Game, where the best junior players in the country are trying to impress the scouts in their draft year.

So I whisper to Don, "I told Lanny to bench that guy."

Don says, "Uh oh. That's Bobby's client." It was one of Bobby Orr's guys. Bobby's an agent, and you know how much Don loves Bobby Orr. "Sorry, Don, too late now. He's benched." And Don went along with it.

I did the same thing to Daniel Briere one year in the Prospects Game. And I knew Daniel well. His uncle used to work at the Ottawa Civic Centre, and Daniel would come down to watch our practice when he was young. I would always give him a stick or two.

We put Daniel on a line with two other Quebec League kids, figuring they'd converse better in French. They took a really long shift, and kept carrying the puck instead of getting it deep. So I say, "If you do that again, you'll miss the next shift."

Well, the next shift they have the same chance to get the puck deep, but instead they carry it and do all this fancy stuff. So, when they come off, I say, "You guys get comfortable here. You're sitting."

Don says, "Brian, what are you doing? We can't bench guys in the Prospects Game!"

"Too late, I just did." And so Don went along with it, again. He always did.

One thing I don't think people realize is how hard Don works. They see him on TV every Saturday night and probably think he comes up with that stuff off the top of his head. Don watches more hockey than anyone! He stays up and watches all the west coast games. He researches and prepares a ton for *Coach's Corner*. He's such a character that I think all the work he puts in gets overlooked.

It's crazy how popular he is now. He can't go anywhere. If he went up and sat beside our prime minister, people would ignore the PM and swarm Don for his autograph.

He can't go out, no matter what city it is. One time, we were at a Prospects Game in Kitchener, and I told him I'd wait and take him back to the hotel after practice. Well, somehow this huge group of fans found out he was there, and bombarded him. He was swarmed. I said, "Don, do you want me to get you out of here?" He says, "No, we'll leave when I'm through." He stayed there and signed until every single kid and adult had an autograph. He won't leave. That's the kind of guy he is.

When Brian Smith, my former teammate, who became a sportscaster in Ottawa, was shot and killed, Don wanted to come down for the funeral. But he didn't want anyone to know. I picked him up at the airport, and he came for the funeral, but he stayed in the back. He knew Brian and I were good friends, and he wanted to pay his respects.

He'd do anything for people.

Shortly after he'd retired from playing, he was selling cars. I came down to see him and he says, "I'm quitting this job. I can't sell a car to an old lady and pretend it's a good car when I know it isn't. I can't sell a car to a guy and say 'a little old lady drove it and she only drove it to the store' when that isn't true. I can't do it."

So he quit. He couldn't lie to people. He still can't. He says what he feels. And that's why people love him so much.

Besides, I bet he didn't want to sell those cars when he knew people might get them dirty. He'd rather burn them first!

10

Stopping Mario (The First Memorial Cup)

We were in trouble.

It was a couple of hours before the 1984 Memorial Cup Final in Kitchener and our best two defencemen were hurt.

Brad Shaw had taken a puck in the eye in the last game, and it was swollen shut. Mark Paterson had sprained his ankle badly. The doctor had looked at him and said, "He's done."

But Shaw put on a shield, and declared himself ready. He was a Kitchener boy, and there was no way he was missing that game. And then Paterson walks into the room as the guys are getting dressed, throws his crutches away, and says,

"I didn't play 80 games to watch the Memorial Cup Final. Tape me up."

• • •

Our first trip to the Memorial Cup was six seasons earlier, in BC. It was only my third year coaching the 67's, but we had a really good team—Bobby Smith, Dougie Wilson, Steve Payne. We came back from three goals down in the final to tie it, but ended up losing 6-5 to Barry Beck and New Westminster. Still, we were thrilled to even get there. The next season, we thought we had a really good shot to win it, but we got upset in the playoffs. That was tough. You always wonder how long it will take to get back.

I was still wondering six years later. You know, I've always said everything happens for a reason, and some things are meant to be. That 1984 season is the perfect example of that. So many of the key players on that team could easily have been playing somewhere else. But some strange things happened to bring that team together.

I guess it started with Brad Shaw. We almost lost him before we had him. I had scouted Brad when he was with the Kitchener Rangers Greenshirts, a midget team, and I really liked him. He was a terrific puckhandler. So I told our head scout, Jack Ferguson, who runs our draft, "I want Brad Shaw." Jack said, "Okay, but he's a little guy for a defence-man. We can get him late."

Well, the first few rounds of that year's draft go by, and about the fifth round, I say to Jack, "I don't want to miss that Shaw kid." Jack says, "We'll get him later." The sixth round goes by. We don't take Shaw. The seventh round goes by. We don't take Shaw. Now it's the eighth round and I'm sweating. So I say, "Okay, Jack. I know Shaw is a little guy. But I'm telling you right now that if he's still there when it's our pick this round, WE'RE TAKING HIM! If he's not there, you and I will talk later."

Luckily for Jack, and our team, he was still there. So we draft Brad Shaw in the eighth round. Well, he comes out of the stands and down to our table, and the guy is pretty big, almost six-feet tall! He's had a growth spurt! Jack looks at him, looks at me, and says sheepishly, "Uhh, he's a little bigger than I thought."

Brad came to our camp the next fall and he was pure magic. Unbelievable. On day one, I said to him, "Tell your family to pack all your clothes. You'll be staying here."

Brad Shaw would become one of the best defencemen to ever play for the 67's.

His defence partner, Mark Paterson, was the perfect complement to Shaw. Brad was an amazing stickhandler, and Mark was a tough, stay-at-home defenceman. He owned the corners and he owned the front of the net.

Mark was from Nepean, and I'd watched him a lot when he was young. I wanted him in the draft, but couldn't get him. He went in the first round to Belleville. He ended up in Ottawa only because another player made a big mistake.

Ali Butorac was our first-round pick in 1980. He was a tough kid with a lot of talent. How tough? Quick story. We were playing up in Kitchener one time, and there had been some noise in our hotel. We found out later some guy had been doing drugs and, I guess, dealing them out of his hotel room. So people were coming in and out of his room, and hammering on the door and making all sorts of noise.

Ali had gone out with Randy Boyd and Randy Cunney-worth just before curfew to get food, and on the way back in, they run into these three guys banging away on this guy's door. Our guys say, "Guys, could you keep it down? We have our hockey team that has to go to bed and get some sleep." Well, those others said the wrong thing back, so Ali calmly hands the food to Cunney and Boyd and says, "Hold this for me, guys."

Bing! Bam! Boom! All three of them were down. Randy Boyd came to my room and told me. "You wouldn't believe what I saw, Coach. Ali took all of them down and out in no time."

So, Ali was the real deal, and I liked him a lot. But he was different. He liked to do things his own way. And that cost him.

One night we got beat 8- or 9-0 in an exhibition game, right in our own rink. So the next morning, I'm giving them a hard skate. Ali comes up to me and says, "I'm not having any fun out here."

I said, "You know what, Ali, for 60 minutes on the bench last night watching you guys play, I didn't have any fun, either."

On the next drill I'm trying to get them to skate hard up ice with the puck, but Ali starts dicking around. He's playing with the puck, kicking it with his feet, making a mockery of the drill.

I yell, "This isn't a fun drill! Get serious!" Ali skates over and says, "Coach, this practice isn't for me. I'm not having any fun. I'm getting off."

I said, "Ali, if you get off, you aren't coming back."

"Well, I'm going home," he says. And he left the ice.

So I go straight to my trainer and say, "Ali is going home. You take my car, take him home to get his stuff, drive him to the airport and wait as long it takes to get him on a flight out of here."

I gather everyone at centre ice and say, "Ali is now on his way home to the Soo. Anyone want to join him?"

They didn't.

That afternoon, Mav (Larry Mavety, the coach and GM of the Belleville Bulls) calls and says, "I hear you sent Ali home. I'm interested. Do you still want Mark Paterson?"

Paterson didn't want to play for Belleville, and had been looking for a trade. You bet I still wanted him.

"Perfect," I tell Mav. "Let's do it."

Ali calls me later that night and says, "Brian, I'm really sorry. I'm ready to come back now."

I say, "Ali, you'll be coming back, but to Belleville because I've traded you there."

Click.

We didn't announce the deal for a few days because Mav was going to trade Ali to Oshawa right away. They really wanted him, and Mav got back a bunch of players he needed. So Ali went to Oshawa, but he ended up back in Belleville to finish his junior career.

About 10 years later, we're up in the Soo, sitting on the bus, waiting to leave after a game. It's dark, and this tough-looking character comes up to the bus and he's looking in the windows. I get off the bus, and it's Ali. He just wanted to say hello. I've seen him many times since. There were no hard feelings.

Anyway, that's how we got Mark Paterson. And Mark Paterson ended up being one of the main reasons we got to the Memorial Cup in 1984.

Paterson and Shaw were part of a really strong defence. We also had Bruce Cassidy, who was identical to Shaw offensively. On the power play together, they were unstoppable. Cassidy's partner was Roy Myllari. And we had Bob Giffen and Todd Clarke as our fifth and sixth defencemen. It was a great group.

But we still needed a goalie.

Belleville had this kid named Darren Pang, who was an Ottawa boy, and one of the most amazing athletes I've ever seen. He was 5-foot-nothin' in elevator shoes, but, boy, was he good. So, I called Mav, and traded him a really good winger named Brian Small for Pang.

Darren Pang (Ottawa 67's goalie, 1982–84): *Larry Mavety called me out of school and asked me to come to his house. He sits me down in the kitchen and says, "Short-ass (that was his nickname for me), I have two places I could trade you. One is Windsor..." Well, my face dropped when he said that. I didn't want to go to Windsor. Then he paused for a minute and said, "... and the other is Ottawa." If only someone had a picture of my eyes lighting up when he said Ottawa. He was having fun with me. He knew I would love to go to Ottawa, and he already knew he was trading me there. So he picks up the phone and calls Killer. He hands me the phone and Killer says, "Pang, I know you're a cocky kid. We have a game in Kingston tonight. Should I play you or would you rather sit on the bench and get to know the guys?" I said, "Killer, you traded for me, I'm playing!"*

I had been in an awful state in Belleville. I wasn't playing well. I was listening to depressing music. Mav was all over me. This was a huge confidence boost that Killer wanted me.

The day of the trade, the guys were really downcast. Brian Small was one of the most popular guys in the room. I brought him down on the bus to Kingston where Mav was going to pick him up, and drop off Pang for me. That bus ride was really quiet. The team wasn't happy about the trade.

So I put Pang in net that night in Kingston. Our team played lousy, but Pang was unbelievable! He stopped everything. And we won. So on the bus after, Pang is a hero. He's holding court at the back of the bus, and everyone is gathered around him. That's how quickly he won them over and they forgot Brian Small!

From that moment on, Pang was our star goalie, and maybe the most popular guy on the team. He was so bubbly, he lit up a room. I never had to give the team pep talks—Pang would do it for me. He never thought we would lose a game, never thought he would give up a goal. That's how confident he was.

I loved getting him riled up. He'd give up a goal, and in the room, I'd say, "Nice goal, Pang."

He'd jump up and say, "Didn't you see it deflect in?!" He'd point at one of his defencemen, "Tell him it went in off your stick! Tell him!" I already knew that, but it was too much fun watching him get worked up.

Boy, Pang took some abuse. I used to tell him it's tough having to bring a highchair to restaurants for him. His roommates on the road would say, "Coach, you can save a bed—just get us a single and Panger can sleep in the drawer."

Doug Wilson told me a story about when Pang was his goalie in Chicago in the NHL a few years later. They were playing Montreal, and Larry Robinson skated by Doug in warm-up and said, "Hey, where's the other half of your goalie?"

One of the funniest moments from that year we went to the Memorial Cup was when Panger and his backup, Greg Coram, came to me and said, "Coach, our warm-ups are awful. The guys are shooting high and missing the nets and we're not getting warmed up."

Players often forget the warm-up is for the goalies. They are superstitious and have a routine where they want to get a certain number of goals. So, the next night we're playing at home, and I go into the room before warm-up and say, "Boys, I know some of you have a quota of goals you have to get in warm-up, so many in the top corner, the bottom corner, off the crossbar. I'm going to let you go out and get your quota. Get them in a hurry, because the goalies are going to sit in here with me until you get them. The warm-ups are for goalies to feel the puck, not to be ducking headshots. So all you guys who need your goals, go get them. When you're ready to have a proper warm-up, I'll let the goaltenders come out."

So out they went, and Pang, Coram and I stayed in the room.

About five minutes went by, and Brad Shaw wanders back in. Now Brad was a real serious guy, but he had a dry sense of humor, too. He ducks his head in the room and says, "Uh, Coach, the guys got their quotas. Can we have a goalie now?"

We won the game, and Pang and Coram said after, "That was the best warm-up we ever had!"

So our backend was really strong that season. Up front, our big line was Adam Creighton, Gary Roberts and Donnie McLaren.

When we drafted Adam Creighton, Jack Ferguson thought he might be able to get him in the second round. I said, "Maybe, Jack. But I know for sure we can take him right now in the first." (I gave Jack a hard time, but he was a great scout.)

So we took Adam in the first round. He was a big gangly kid out of Welland, and he wasn't a very graceful skater. He had trouble standing up the first year. He was just so awkward, he would fall down all the time, especially on face-offs. But I had played pro against his Dad, Dave, and I saw something in Adam I really liked.

Adam was one of those guys who wanted nothing else in life but to be a hockey player. He probably came further in his years here than anyone I've ever coached.

Adam Creighton (Ottawa 67's forward, 1981–85): *He was talking to reporters after one game my first year, and they asked him why he ever took me in the first round. Killer answered, "Can't you see? He's going to be the strongest player in the league. He keeps having to pick himself up off the ice. He's doing 150 push-ups a game!"*

I remember his first year. Walking out to our bench from the dressing room, you had to come around the corner of the rink right past where our owner Howard Darwin sat. And there was always this group of fans who would heckle me. They'd say, "Killer, why don't you just get out of here! And take that Creighton kid with you!"

I knew Howard was hearing it, too.

But Adam worked incredibly hard and he kept getting better. By about the midway point of his rookie season, those same hecklers would yell, "Kilrea, why don't you get out of here!" They had dropped the part about taking Creighton with me.

By the time 1984 came around, Adam was a star. And with Roberts and McLaren, it was a formidable top line.

But there was one thing I thought we were still missing. We needed a little more toughness up front. Remember how Mav had called me when I sent Ali home, and we made a deal? Well, this time I got word that Mav had sent home one of his players, a kid named Richard Adolfi.

So I called Mav in Belleville and said, "What happened?"

Mav said, "Well, he was jacking up the tires on a car, and the police caught him."

It sounds bad, but that wasn't the whole story. You see Mav had this buddy named Russ, who all the kids on the Bulls team knew well. They were messing with his car as a practical joke. But the police happened to show up and Richard was the one who was caught. Mav was in a tough spot. He'd had some other troubles in Belleville and he had told his kids, "The next guy who breaks curfew or does anything else is going home." So Richard was sent home. Mav was really a big softie. He would have brought him back eventually, but I saw an opportunity.

So I said to Mav, "Richard won't do you any good at home. Would you trade him to me?"

Mav said he'd think about it for a day. So I called Richard and said, "If I traded for you, would you report?" He said, "Sure."

Mav and I talked the next day and he said, "Okay, I'll do it. Just give me a draft pick." So, I ended up getting the tough forward I wanted in Richard Adolfi. But I still had to go to our other owner, Earl Montagano.

I said, "Earl, I made a deal. I got a player named Richard Adoplhi from Belleville. He'd been suspended."

Earl said, "What had he been suspended for?"

"For jacking up a car and taking the tires off." You should have seen Earl's face. So I explained the rest of the story. Earl still looked worried. He said, "What are you going to do with him?"

I said, "Well, Earl, the first thing I'm going to do is take away his jack."

He stared at me blankly for a minute, then we broke up laughing. Fortunately, Earl got my twisted humour.

Richard Adolfi would end up playing a significant role when we made it to the Memorial Cup.

That's how some of the key pieces came together on that team. But there was one other important event that year. I was chosen to coach Canada at the World Juniors in Sweden.

It was a real thrill. Back then, the tournament was just a round robin. You played every team once. We had a chance at gold, but we needed to beat Russia in our second-last game. We tied them 3-3. Because we'd lost to Finland, they had the silver, so our last game was for bronze against the Czechs. It's tough to get Canadians up for bronze, when they almost had a shot at gold. So we lost, and finished fourth. But I learned a lot watching those European teams.

I watched how they ran their power plays, sometimes shifting to a high point man, two guys at the side, two guys in front. They always changed things around, and their power plays were always dangerous. They also made me realize a 45-second shift of hard work was enough—that you don't always need to leave your best guys out for a minute or 1:10. I knew this was going to help us in Ottawa.

The day I got back, my pal Billy Patterson, the sportscaster, was there to meet us. I told him we were going to win the Memorial Cup.

• • •

We almost didn't get there, though. The tournament was in Kitchener and we played them in the Ontario League final. Now, back then, they didn't bring an extra team if the host won its league title. Today, we would have automatically been in by making it to the league final, but not then. And to make it even tougher, the circus had been booked in Ottawa, so after the first two games, we had to play the rest in Kitchener. We ended up having to win three there to win the league title. But we did. Adam Creighton dominated, and we were in the Memorial Cup.

Adam Creighton: *John Tucker was their star forward. We had both been drafted by Buffalo the year before, and Scotty Bowman [who ran the Sabres] had come down to watch the games. Killer knew that, and matched me against John. He was already trying to help my pro career. He wanted me to show Scotty I was more than ready to play in the NHL.*

So, it was Ottawa, Kitchener, the Kamloops Oilers from the west, and Laval. And Laval had a certain forward who went by the name of Mario Lemieux.

Mario had destroyed the Quebec League that year.

JD: *He isn't kidding: 133 goals, 149 assists for 282 points in 70 games. That's more than four points a game, for an entire season.*

Our first game was against Mario and Laval on the second day of the tournament. We had a strategy against Mario that I'll explain in a minute. But the start of the game was a disaster. They scored on their first two shots. Mario got one of them. They weren't pretty ... off a skate, off a stick. But we were down 2-0 less than two minutes in. We had to do something.

So we pulled Darren Pang. Remember I told you how bubbly and happy he always was? Well, this was the one exception in his entire career. He was fuming! As he came to the bench, my assistant, Gordie Hamilton, says, "Look at the face on Pang." I said, "I know. Don't even make eye contact with him. Just let him get on the bench and cool off."

I could feel his eyes staring me down. He was banging on the boards and kicking his sticks and throwing stuff everywhere. But we had to do something to wake up our team. So we put Greg Coram in.

Darren Pang: *I did throw quite a fit. I was trying to stare him down. But I was more mad at myself than anyone else. Mario had beat me on a pretty weak shot. I knew it was momentum-sapping for our team. I had played that whole league final series against Kitchener, and here I am on the big stage getting yanked in the first game! I think I was overwhelmed a bit. I remember getting off the bus at the rink and seeing Mario. He was so big and such a presence, I guess it got to me. But after I settled down on the bench, Killer came over and said, "Pang, don't sit here and sulk! Get yourself ready because you are playing the second game!" That gave me my confidence back, knowing he still believed in me. So I sat back and watched Greg Coram stand on his head.*

We had to figure out a way to shut down Mario. You got mesmerized watching the brilliance he possessed. He did things with the puck that were incredible.

We didn't try too hard to match up lines against him, though I preferred having Mark Paterson out there on defence when he was on. We always had one forward chase him everywhere. We told our guys to force him to the wall early, try to finish your checks on him. We didn't think his supporting cast was good enough, so if we got him to give up the puck, we'd be all right. So, the forward would follow him, and the defenceman would force him to the wall and make him give up the puck. Simple enough. And it worked.

He didn't score again, Coram did the job in goal, and we came back to win 6-5.

Brad Shaw (Ottawa 67's defenceman, 1981–84): *I think our balance was what got Mario discouraged. Our top four D all played him very well, and after a while, it just seemed like he gave up. It was almost like he was resigned to the fact they weren't good enough to beat us. I was really surprised at how little he worked once we took control. He just quit. And once he stopped putting 100 per cent in, the rest of them realized they didn't have a chance.*

Mario just didn't have enough help. Quebec lost all three games and were knocked out of the tournament.

The next night we played Kamloops. I put Pang back in and he was terrific. We won 5-1. Cassidy got a couple and Adam Creighton got his second.

One more win and we would go straight to the final. But instead, we lost 7-2 to Kitchener. I think they were still pretty

peeved we'd beaten them at home for the league championship. It was a closer game than that. We had a ton of shots,
but their goalie, Ray LeBlanc, stoned us.

So, we had to beat Kamloops again in the semis. I remember the crowd was all over Adam Creighton. They chanted
"Adam, Adam" every time he touched the puck.

And he touched it a lot. He scored two, and got three
assists and we won 7-2. Adam just dominated. He was taking
over the tournament. That gangly kid who kept falling down
on face-offs that first year had come a long way.

But that was the game we lost Shaw and Paterson. Shaw
took a puck in the eye, and was cut really bad. And Paterson
left the building on crutches. And now we'd have to play
Kitchener again in the final.

The day of the game, I didn't think there was any chance
Paterson would play. But then he limped into that dressing
room, and threw away the crutches, and you knew there
was no stopping him. I'm not even sure how they got his
foot into the boot, it was so swollen. But he went out there
and hit everything in sight.

Shaw put on a shield to protect his eye, but that lasted
all of one shift. He was digging the puck out behind the net,
and someone hit him. I remember he came to the bench and
yelled, "Take this thing off now." So he played the rest of the
game with one eye, and no mask.

Brad Shaw: *I got El-Kabonged, and being the proud player that
I was, I blamed the visor. So I tossed it. I just felt better without it.*

A bad eye was not going to stop me from playing in the Memorial Cup Final in my hometown. When you get bypassed by your hometown team in the draft, over and over, it sticks with you. So, I really wanted to show them they had made a mistake. We had to win that game. There was no other option.

Kitchener had some great forwards, but their real star was a big defenseman named Dave Shaw (no relation to Brad). He had a booming shot, and he could hit guys.

That's where Richard Adolfi comes in. Shaw was kind of having his way with our guys, so I said to Richard on the bench, "You go up to that guy and tell him the next time he's going to get tough with one of our players, you are coming to see him."

I kind of assumed Richard would wait until a whistle or a scrum in the corner or something. But he jumps over the boards, and skates right up to Shaw and starts having a talk. The ref blows the whistle and says, "I'm trying to drop the puck here, would you get in position!" But Richard kept on talking.

When he came off, I said, "Richard, you probably could have picked a better time for that. What did you say to him?"

Well, Richard had these funny eyes, they rolled a little when he got mad. He just looked dangerous. He said to me, "Coach, I told him if you touch another one of our players, I'm going to ram this fucking stick down your throat."

I said, "Well, I may not have put it in those words, Richard, but okay."

On his next few shifts, Richard took some hefty runs at Shaw, just so he knew he meant it. And I really think it made a difference. Shaw didn't have his usual game.

Kitchener was a team that would win the game in the first period. They would come out flying. That's what happened in the round-robin game. Our belief was that if we stayed with them in the first, we'd win.

Well, the guy upstairs must have been rooting for us that day. It was just a bizarre game. It was 1-1 when Phil Patterson (no relation to Mark) fired a puck from the corner and it somehow went in to give us the lead. Then, with only a few seconds left in the first period, Bruce Cassidy fired the puck from centre ice into the corner in their end. The goalie went behind his net, ready to play it as it came around, but it hit the stanchion and went in.

Darren Pang: *You could see their bench sag when that puck went in. I think they knew they were done, because we were on fire. We drilled them, we hemmed them in their zone. Our forechecking that day was as relentless as I've ever seen in hockey. It was pretty clear after the first they had nothing left.*

We never looked back. Creighton scored one and was the star of the game. Bruce Cassidy got a pair. Gary Roberts scored on a wild slap that went top corner. (You never knew where a Roberts shot was going.) Even Shaw scored with his one good eye. And Pang was terrific in net.

7-2 Ottawa. We were Memorial Cup Champions.

Boy, it was a proud feeling. I was happiest for our owners, Earl and Howard, but especially Howard. He had been a part of junior hockey for a long time, and this was his first Memorial Cup.

Creighton was tournament MVP. He had outplayed Mario. He had outplayed Tucker from Kitchener. He outplayed everyone. But it was a true team effort: Richard Adolfi, and that little talk he gave to the guy on the other team, Cassidy, Roberts, Donnie McLaren—there were so many heroes. Pang comes back from being pulled against Quebec, and gets voted the best goalie in the tournament. And the unbelievable grit that Shaw and Paterson had showed playing hurt.

Brad Shaw: *You can't imagine what it was like skating around with that trophy in your hometown. I remember trying to lift the trophy. I had separated my shoulder earlier, and was wearing a brace, so I couldn't extend my arms up. Any picture you see of me that day, you'll see the trophy is tilted because I couldn't lift it properly. But winning for Killer is what made the moment special. We knew he had had some great teams that had fallen short before us. To win it for him was truly something. One of the greatest moments of my life.*

I remember the celebration in the dressing room. I had come in after doing all the interviews and one of our guys was outside the room handing out our sticks to anyone who walked by.

I said, "Hey! We will need those again in September!"

I lit up a victory cigar on the bus (the rules were a little different back then). A few of the kids came up and said, "Would you have any more of those, Coach?"

"Sure, I think I have a couple of extra boxes."

So every kid on the team lit up a cigar on that bus. You can imagine the smoke. Most of them didn't last long. There was a lot of coughing going on.

But I sure savoured mine.

11

The Boys on the Bus

People used to say to me, especially in my last years of coaching, "Aren't you sick of those long bus trips?"

Sick of them? I loved them.

I always told my owners, "You are paying me to see Ontario." When you drive from Ottawa to Sault Ste. Marie, you can't believe how many beautiful sights there are. It's the same with Barrie, Sarnia, Windsor ... all of them. We've seen the province, end to end. If you keep saying, "When are we going to get there?" then the bus rides feel long. If you just enjoy the natural beauty around you, you get there in no time.

But the company helps, too. And boy, did I have some company.

Jeff Hunt: *The first year I bought the team, I went on every road trip. If only I'd brought a tape recorder. It was like some TV show, some warped Seinfeld, listening to Killer and the cast of characters he had with him.*

The Cast

TANK

Tank's real name was Gordie Hetherington, but he's always been Tank. Please, don't ever ask him how he got the nickname, because when Tank tells you a story, you're likely to fall asleep before he finishes. By the time he was 19, he was well over 6 feet and 200 pounds, so you can pretty much figure out why he was called Tank.

Tank was with me from day one. I grew up playing baseball against him, so we were always friends. When I got the job with the 67's, he asked if there was anything he could do. He was semi-retired, so he could make all the road trips. Tank came on every one.

It was his job to get the tickets for every game, and distribute them to the players. We get a certain number of tickets for each away game, and kids always have family and friends in each town, so Tank would make sure everyone got their tickets.

Jeff Hunt: *Tank would make the first list, then Killer would take it and mark it up with a red marker, like a teacher. Killer always had the last word.*

Tank would also arrange for the food after the game, so when the kids got on the bus, it was waiting for them. And the coolers. Tank made sure the coolers were stocked with pops and water for the boys, and maybe some cold ones for the grown-ups.

Jeff Hunt: *One time, someone new on the bus was trying to be helpful and loaded up the cooler. Big mistake. Tank was fuming. He took it off the bus, dumped it in the parking lot, and reloaded it himself. No one else packs Tank's cooler.*

We loved to mess with Tank. One time, up in the Soo, we had a long trip back, so I told him to order extra subs for the kids. Let's say there were 30 of us on the bus, I think I told him to order 50 subs. The kids would eat a sub-and-a-half on a trip like that. So, Tank comes on the bus with all the subs, and he's really pleased with himself. He says, "I got a really good deal."

So Bobby (you'll meet Bobby in a minute) starts passing them out, and he gets about halfway through the bus and comes back up front. "We're out of subs," he says. Turns out Tank had got only 50 halves instead of fulls. No wonder it was so cheap! We turned the bus around and went back. We only ribbed him about that for a few ... years. "Hey, Tank, remember that great deal you got us on those subs!"

The first year Jeff bought the team we had some real fun with Tank.

Jeff Hunt: *We decided to tell Tank that as a new owner, I was going to change things up and customize the food orders. I told him, "We're going to let every guy decide what he wants to eat." So if Brian Campbell wants McDonald's, Dan Tessier wants Subway and Nick Boynton wants pizza, they'd all get it. We knew this would rock Tank's world. In the past, 10 pepperoni, 10 cheese was about as complicated as the orders got. So I tell Tank and his face just goes blank.*

JD: *Killer is laughing, to the point of crying, recalling this story.*

Poor Tank! His head was spinning. He was grumbling. I think he wanted to kill us. But he took the orders . . . pizza for one guy, Colonel Sanders for the next guy . . . we finally had to tell him, before he lost it.

Tank is the best. He would never get into a debate. He'd just sigh and take it.

STUMP

Stump (Gary Craig) was my buddy since I was a kid. We played hockey together, played ball together, bummed school together, quit school together. He went on to work for the city, installing water meters and doing plumbing. He could do anything. So he came along on the road trips and was like an assistant trainer. He'd make sure all the equipment was in the bus, he'd man one door on the bench during games, just do all the odd jobs a hockey team on the road needs.

Stump was pretty famous around Ottawa for his fights. When he was young, he'd rather fight than eat.

One time at a bar in Hull, some guy said the wrong thing to Stump, so he took care of him. The police showed up, and they chased Stump out the back. He was trying to scale a wire fence when they grabbed him by the belt. His pants came down, but they wouldn't go over his shoes. So they dragged Stump back through the club with his pants around his ankles, and threw him in the paddy wagon. My Dad and I had to bail him out. We bailed out Stump a lot.

Another time, Stump was in a restaurant, Jimmy's Grill on Bank Street, with Grant Edmonds, another pal of ours. Four guys came in, and they were looking for trouble. Stump gave them a look, and one guy said, "What are you looking at?" Stump said, "Not much." Well, the next thing you know they were all outside. But it was four on two, and Grant wasn't much of a fighter, so the four won.

Stump never forgot. A year later, he found out where each one of them lived, and got them, one at a time. He waited in the shadows for them to come home. You didn't want to mess with Stump.

He didn't lose much, except to Jerry Barber. Jerry ran The Chaudiere across the river in Hull. Stump went over and fought him three straight nights. He kept losing, and he kept going back for more.

Stump (Gary Craig): *Wasn't anyone that beat Jerry Barber. He was the toughest man I ever ran in to. He was about 250 and built like a brick shithouse. But I kept going back, and finally he said, "This is crazy." He got tired of beating me up so we became friends.*

Tank and Stump would go over to Hull together and it was like an old Western. Tables and chairs would get thrown. That was when they were young. But they stayed tough all their life. You wouldn't want to say anything bad about the Ottawa 67's to Stump.

Stump: *I chased a guy out of the rink in Kingston once. He was always bad-mouthing our players from the stands, calling them sucks. He wouldn't shut up. So between periods, I chased him right out of the rink. He's still there, too, the peckerhead. And now my grandson is playing in Kingston, and I'm going to have to see the guy all the time!*

Stump and Tank would tell their stories on the bus, and the kids in the back would start creeping up towards the front to listen.

The players would say, "I think I can take you, Stump." Stump would go back and arm-wrestle them. They loved it. He'd show them how to fight, too. Some nights, I didn't give the team a pep talk. Stump would go back and fire them up.

Jim Fox (Ottawa 67's forward, 1977–80): *Stump was like a drill sergeant. He would walk up and down the aisles yelling at guys.*

Stump: *Sure, I'd give them crap when they didn't play good. They were so well looked after by the 67's, and then they play like a bunch of assholes? When they got it, they deserved it.*

Jim Fox: *Stump, Tank—these guys weren't just characters, they were almost cartoon characters. The bus rides were sometimes more entertaining than the games.*

BERT

I met Bert O'Brien soon after I started coaching. I started with tykes, then bantams, and when I graduated to midget, Bert was one of the guys who ran the league. My second year of midget, I joined South Ottawa and Bert was the manager of the team. He and his wife, Kathy, never had kids, so their way to give back was to volunteer in hockey. They'd do anything for the kids. When I first went to the 67's, Bert started coaching junior B, and won eight championships in 10 years. So when I came back from the Islanders, I called him and asked him to coach with me.

Bert still had a full-time job, so he said, "Let me think about it. When do I have to make my decision?" I said, "Oh, about an hour, because that's when I'm going to introduce you at the press conference."

Bert O'Brien: *I'm sitting in my office, next door to the company president's office, thinking, "Coaching the 67's with Killer, this is great!" Then I realize, this is going to be in the papers. I'm going to have to tell my boss. So, I sat there trying to get up enough nerve to tell the boss I had to go because I was taking a second job coaching the 67's.*

Luckily, Bert said yes, and we've been together ever since. Best assistant and friend a guy could have.

I don't know how Bert did it. He was still working full time with Mechron Power Systems while he was helping me coach the 67's. We wouldn't get in from road trips some Sunday nights until 2:00 or 3:00 in the morning, and Bert would go to work at 6:30 a.m. One night, we had bad weather coming back from the Soo. Bert got off the bus and went straight to work!

BOBBY

Bobby's job on the bus was running the VCR. Later, it was the DVD player. I'd let the kids choose the movies most of the time, but I won't stand for those stupid ones. When they put those on, I'd threaten to put on *Columbo*. Or I'd just turn up my Anne Murray music so they couldn't hear the movie. We liked *Slap Shot*, though. We'd never take that one off.

Bobby's real job was being our video guy. I met him through my cousins, Gordie and Bruce Hamilton. They ran the Ottawa Sooners football team, and Bobby did their video. So he'd do it for them in the summer, and us in the winter. He'd tape all the games for us, break down the power play and penalty kill. Bobby was also a real Mr. Fix-It. He could fix anything. Whatever job you gave Bobby, he got it done. The kids would make up songs about him. Everybody loved Bobby.

THE TRAINER

We had some characters for trainers, too.

Brian Sardoz was one. Once, on the bus, he bet us he could put a whole orange in his mouth and swallow it. He did it, too. He'd win all sorts of bets. He could also take a full glass of beer, just open his throat, and it was gone. He used to always drink for free 'cause he would bet guys he could drink a beer faster than them. They never had a chance. It was gone in a second. He used to work in the oil sands out west, and once this guy bet him he wouldn't swim across this cesspool of crap and pee, and the worst stuff you could think of. So Brian swam across. They made him sit in the back of the truck on the way back to town, he smelled so bad.

Jeff Keech was another trainer, one of my favorites. He was a young guy, and liked to go out. One day, we're in Kingston and we can't find Keech. Word came down that he was lying on the medical table in the other team's room. He wasn't feeling well. So the Kingston trainer took care of both teams that night. On the way home, our doctor, Peter Premachuk, is on the bus. He comes up and whispers to me, "Jeff wants to go to the hospital in Brockville." I say, "Doc, do you think there's any chance he'll die between here and Ottawa?"

"No."

So, I say, "Good. He can wait till we get home." We dropped him off at the Queensway-Carleton Hospital, and went to the rink. Five minutes later, Keech shows up.

"They just gave me a couple of hangover pills," he says.

And he wanted me to stop the bus to go to the hospital!

The trainers changed a bit over the years, but the rest of the crew stayed the same. I'd sit in the front row, on the side opposite the driver. Bert would sit across from me, behind the driver. The other assistant, Vince Malette, or whoever it was at the time, would sit behind me. Bobby sat behind Vince. Tank would sit behind Bert. Stump would sit behind Tank.

Jeff Hunt: *You would not believe the conversations. Just taking a food order would be as complicated as, like, saving the rain forest. The banter was hilarious. We'd be two hours outside of North Bay, and they'd be arguing over what we were going to eat. They'd go back and forth, tempers would flare, then Killer would snap. All over pizza or burgers!*

Then there was the time coming home from Oshawa when they made the horrific discovery that they were low on inventory. There wasn't enough beer to make it home. So Killer had to do forensic accounting to figure out how this had happened.

We had to figure out who had how many. You had to get to the bottom of it. So, we'd go through the math. "Bobby had two, Bert had one, Stump didn't have any ..." (Stump didn't like beer.) You didn't want to ask Tank, because Tank used to work in the government for John Diefenbaker, so he knew how to take 10 minutes to answer a question. Tank would say, "Well, let's see, I was having one, but then I had to go to the back and talk to ..." You'd be asleep in no time listening to Tank.

There would be some disagreement. "Bobby didn't have two, he had three!" We needed to know where they all went. Running out of beer on the bus home was not acceptable.

Mike Futa (former GM, Owen Sound Attack): *I remember the first time Killer invited me up to his hotel room for a beer. There were all these guys there around Killer and he was holding court, telling stories. And I just kept thinking, this is Don Corleone! And these are his made men! Killer told me everybody had a job. One guy was in charge of the orange cooler, the other guy had the other cooler. And sure enough, the next morning, out they'd walk—the guy in charge of the orange cooler had his cooler, the other guy had his cooler, everybody doing their thing.*

We had great times on those bus trips, except for the couple of times we almost died.

We were leaving Belleville after an exhibition game. We were on the 401, and I'm looking ahead at the road, and I notice the bus is veering towards the right. The tires are starting to kick up stones from the shoulder and you could hear the noise of the stones hitting the underside of the bus. So, I say to the driver, "Is there something wrong with the bus?" He says, "No, it's me." Those were his last words. He passed out. His head fell forward onto the steering wheel.

I had two choices: run to the back of the bus and hope, or grab the wheel. So I dragged him quickly out of the driver's seat, and grabbed the wheel. I had some truck driving experience and I had learned not to jerk the wheel too hard. We were coming towards a tree line, and maybe 15 feet from the tree line, I was able to get it stopped. The bus was leaning over in a ditch, almost on its side. I got all the guys to stand on the high side, and we got them off, one by one. I was the captain of the ship. I got off last.

Bert O'Brien: *The first guy who jumped out was the trainer. And when he opened the door, the cooler fell out and everything inside it rolled down into the ditch. Tank says in horror, "The cooler!" Losing the cooler and its contents ... that was an emergency for us. So, Stump and I get down in the ditch on our hands and knees looking for the contents, one can at a time!*

A couple of weeks later, we're driving up to North Bay on a Sunday. And the same driver shows up! We were a little leery, but he'd been cleared, so we figured he must be OK.

This time Jeff Hunt and his brother Alec are sitting right behind the driver. We went through Petawawa, and were just past Deep River. I was busy doing the lineup for the game. I felt us drifting off to one side, and then I heard Jeff's brother yell. The driver had passed out again!

Jeff grabbed the wheel and steered, and I jumped down on the floor to handle the brake pedal with my hand. We were lucky to be on a stretch of open highway, because we were veering all over it. There was a steep down slope just a couple of hundred yards ahead, but we stopped it just before we got there. They sent us a new bus and driver from North Bay. That was the last time we saw the driver. Thankfully.

Besides those two close calls, the bus trips were great. I miss them. But it was time. For the crew, too. We're all getting up there, now. Stump is 75, like me. Tank is 84. He had a heart attack up in Sudbury a few years ago, and the doctors recommended he stop going on the road trips. He wasn't happy. But the rest of us were only a few years behind him.

I couldn't even try to calculate the number of hours we spent on buses over all those years. But I never minded. Touring Ontario with your friends, going from hockey game to hockey game. Anne Murray with you the whole way. How could anyone ever complain about that?

12

Long Nights on Long Island

I loved coaching junior hockey.

I would have been perfectly content spending my entire career with the 67's. But once in a while, NHL teams would call to see if I might be interested.

During our Memorial Cup run in 1984, Gerry Ehman, the head scout for the New York Islanders, came down and wanted to have a talk.

They had been watching me for years. Gerry said Al Arbour was thinking of stepping down soon, and would I be interested in replacing him.

That was a tough one. I loved Ottawa, loved coaching the kids. But I said, "Sure, I'm always willing to listen."

We won the Memorial Cup and went down to Daytona Beach for a week, just as a reward to the team. The Islanders called me again down there, and said they were really interested and wanted to get something done.

So when we got back from Florida, I flew to Long Island and met with Gerry and Bill Torrey, the Islanders' president. They told me Al was thinking of retiring that year or next. They wanted me to start as his assistant and then take over after he stepped down.

The Islanders had just come off winning four straight Stanley Cups. This was a great team and a great franchise. I had some thinking to do.

So I called Don Cherry.

When Don had been offered the coaching job in Boston years before, he was in Montreal and he called me. He said, "I need to talk to you right now."

I hung up the phone, grabbed my keys and drove to Montreal, without even knowing what it was about. If Don needed to talk, that was enough. I betcha from the time I got the call to the time I was in his room wasn't two-and-a-half hours. Don wanted my advice then about whether he should take the Bruins job, and now I needed his.

So this time, I called Don. He told me not to take the job.

"You're not an assistant coach," he said. "You shouldn't go anywhere where you're not the head coach."

I listened. But I took the job anyway.

I didn't mind being an assistant coach to a guy like Al Arbour. I knew him from the days I'd played with and against him, and I respected him, both as a player and as a coach. I figured I'd learn from Al the first year, and then take over. But it didn't turn out that way.

Before I get to what went wrong, I'll say this. I gained a lot from my time there. I learned from Al Arbour. Watching him, his drills, it was like getting a refresher course on coaching from one of the best ever.

Al didn't get mad. He always tried to understand and give his players a full vote of confidence. He always focused on the positive when they were in a bad stretch. And we had some bad stretches those two years.

The biggest difference between junior and the pros is that you don't have to teach. With the kids in junior, you teach them how to pass. Well, the pros know how to pass. You teach the kids how to shoot. These guys know how to shoot. So, in junior, you are forever teaching them things to make them better players. In the National League, the players better already know it, because if they don't, someone else who does will take their place. You coach in the NHL, you don't teach.

Boy, did they have some players to coach. The stuff they could do, you wouldn't believe. My good friend Gord Hamilton came down for a weekend to see us play two games. Mike Bossy had a hat trick in each one. He scored from every position on the ice. And the way Trottier got him the puck no matter where he was ... Gord was just blown away. He'd never seen anything like it.

They had some characters, too. Butch Goring was a funny guy. So was Billy Smith. Except on game days. On game days, no one could speak to Billy. And I mean NO ONE. You just stayed away. He was one of the most intense guys I'd ever seen.

They had some great players, but there is a fine line between winning and losing. And we were losing more than winning. The dynasty was over.

I would never end up becoming head coach on Long Island.

Al didn't retire after the first year, and in the second year, things went a little south.

They felt I was too close to the players, which maybe I was. I would have some players come to my house to look at video. The players wanted to get better, and I lived right on their way home. So I thought it would be good for some of them. They could get away from the rink and I could point out some of the mistakes they made.

Bob Bourne (New York Islanders forward, 1974–86): *We'd play an away game, in New York or Philly, and when we got back, Killer's wife would always have a five-gallon bucket of beer on ice. We were always welcome there. We'd sit around, and he'd talk to us about the philosophy of hockey. I learned so much from him.*

But Bill Torrey didn't like it. He told me, "Al Arbour has never had a player at his house."

I said, "He doesn't know what he's missing." Maybe it wasn't the right response, but it was how I felt.

I think the final straw came one night on a road trip. We had lost a few games, and I was in a meeting with all the scouts. They were talking about how some of the veterans were letting Al down.

I spoke up and said, "We're always picking on the same guys. The stars. When do we start picking on the guys who aren't doing anything?"

And Gerry Ehman, who was my backer when they hired me, got really mad.

"If you can do a better job of scouting, go ahead!" he said.

I said, "That's not the point. We're picking on the guys who got us there. They aren't getting any help."

So I left, and on the way up to my room, I ran into Mike Bossy and Bryan Trottier. They asked me where I was going, and I said, "I'm going to watch a replay of the game to find the mistakes."

They asked, "Can we watch it?" And I said, "Sure."

So Bossy and Trottier came to my room, ordered a club sandwich and a glass of milk from room service, and we watched the game together.

Bryan Trottier (New York Islanders forward, 1975–90, Hall-of-Famer): *He didn't just do that on the road. He'd yank us into the coaches' office quite often to look at our power play, or our forecheck. He wasn't picking favorites, he was picking our brains. We loved it. We loved him. He was very respectful of the veterans. He wanted our input.*

The next morning, Bill Torrey said, "I hear you had someone in your room last night?" I said, "Yes, two players. I thought it was a good idea."

"Well, Al never does that."

I walked into the restaurant and all the scouts were on one side and there were no seats left. They were having a meeting, and I guess they didn't tell me about it.

So, one of the players, Bobby Bourne, gets up and says, "Killer, why don't you come over here and sit with us, your friends." And I did.

I knew then it was almost over for me on Long Island.

Bob Bourne: *I remember him walking into that restaurant, and they had no place for him to sit. He looked so embarrassed. I stood up right away, and asked him to come sit with us. I loved Brian Kilrea. I would go through a wall for him. He didn't deserve that.*

The final straw came when an article came out in the paper about one of our defencemen, Gordie Lane. They were thinking of sending him down, but I was arguing against it. Gordie was a real hard worker, he was tough in front of the net, and both goalies liked him for that.

We got back from a road trip and there was a story in the paper about Gordie. He was praising me, saying I was one of the main reasons he was still here.

I got to the rink that day and Bill Torrey said, "I see you're getting a lot of ink, Killer." He wasn't happy.

I said, "I didn't say anything to the paper. I don't write the stories."

At the end-of-the-year banquet, I knew it was over. I had a two-year contract, and they weren't going to renew it. And I was fine with that. We were sitting at a table in this beautiful restaurant, with all the coaches and management people. And again, Bobby Bourne comes over and says, "Killer, the players would like you to come sit with them."

So I got up and left the table. And that was the end of my time on Long Island.

Don Cherry: *I could see it comin' from the time he called me and asked if he should take the job. I told him the players would love him, and Al Arbour and Bill Torrey wouldn't like it. I mean, the players came and sang Christmas carols at his house, that's how much they respected Brian. He was just not meant to be an assistant coach. I wish he had waited and gotten the right offer to be a head coach in the NHL. He would have been as big as Bruce Boudreau is now. Times three.*

I had no hard feelings. I think Bill Torrey liked me, but didn't think I was the right guy. They thought they were getting this really tough coach, aloof from the players. And that wasn't me.

But I have no regrets. Some people go back to school to get an MBA. I took a two-year sabbatical from junior, and got a refresher course in coaching. And those players were a great bunch of guys. The other teams had just caught up with them.

Al Arbour would coach one more year, and then Terry Simpson would come in to replace him. And I was more than happy to go back to Ottawa.

Bryan Trottier: *I was disappointed. I think we all were. We thought Brian was being groomed to be Al's replacement. I think he would have been a breath of fresh air. Who knows what would have happened if he had gotten to be the head coach? I think things might have gone differently for our organization. But they hired Terry Simpson, and he was something much different than Killer would have been. And it didn't work out very well.*

Bob Bourne: *If Killer had stayed on and become the head coach, we would have won more Stanley Cups. I truly believe that.*

The National League would come calling again. Chicago called a few times, but the hardest one for me was Toronto.

A few years after my stop on Long Island, George Armstrong had decided he wanted to stop coaching the Maple

Leafs. He called me and asked if I would be interested in replacing him.

Hmm. This was a tough one. I could have been the coach of the Toronto Maple Leafs. And I liked Harold Ballard. He did a lot of stuff behind the scenes for charity. I figured he might be a lot like Eddie Shore. And if I survived Eddie, I could survive Harold.

This was August. I called Bert, my assistant, and we talked about it. I was torn. But I couldn't go. I had already told my players I would be there, and I didn't want to do that to my team. I had already left the 67's once. I couldn't do it again.

So George Armstrong called and said, "Mr. Ballard and I will come up tonight to get the contract done."

And I said, "Sorry, George, I just can't do that to my players."

They ended up bringing in Doug Carpenter from Cornwall.

Who knows if things would have worked out in Toronto. I don't think about those kinds of things. Some people love the NHL life, the nice hotels, the charter planes. But I love junior, love the bus rides. It's a great life.

The NHL life today, they have it too good. I think everyone in the NHL should have to play for Eddie Shore for one year.

Then they'd all know how good they have it.

13

You Got Three Options!

When I was trying to get a point across to a player, I would often tell them, "You got three options. Do what I say or . . ." Well, I can't repeat the other two. But they're the same, and they aren't too polite.

Mark Edmundson (Ottawa 67's forward, 1992–95): *This may be the phrase Killer is known best for. This story has been told in every hockey league there is. My second year in Ottawa, we had this big tall defenceman from Halifax named Mike Johnson. Killer always picked on one or two guys the most, and that year, Mike was the target. One game, we were up by a couple of goals when Mike skated around the back of our net and* *threw a pass right up the middle. The other team picked it off and scored. You could see the smoke coming out of Killer's ears. So we go into the dressing room between periods and we know he's going to lose his mind. Mike had sat in the same stall for three years, but when Killer came in, he was so worked up, he couldn't find where Johnson was sitting. He was looking all around the room for him. Finally, he sees him and says, "Johnson, you got three options! You can shoot the puck hard off the glass. You can f*#! off! Or you can f*#! off! And he stormed out of the room. We burst out laughing. I've seen Mike Johnson a few times over the years and the first thing I always say is, "Johnson, you got three options!"*

JD: *Every single 67's player I interviewed has their own "You got three options" story. The names, and mistakes, are different. But the punchline remains pretty much the same.*

I could be tough on guys sometimes, but it was always for their benefit. My philosophy is that you are always trying to improve, whether it's hockey, baseball, golf, anything.

When you are coaching, you coach to win, but you also coach knowing full well this is a stepping stone for some of these kids. So, what you are hoping to do is, while you are winning, you are improving them, you are getting them ready for the next step.

They don't realize when they join you at 16 how tough it is to become a pro. They see it on TV and it doesn't look as fast as it really is. They have all been stars all the way up to junior, and they think they are going to jump into the TV and become a National League player. Well, they don't know what it takes to become a National League player. They have no idea! You've got to get bigger, stronger, better.

And you have to be disciplined. I've always said the key to everything is discipline—on and off the ice. You can't think you are going to be able to play your best if you aren't ready to be disciplined. That means staying within the system, being a team player. You have to give away your individuality. Sure, you can use your individual skills to get the puck to the net. But when it comes to getting the puck out of your own end, and all the other things that help teams win, you need to work as a unit to get them done. So, discipline means sacrificing yourself for the good of the team. Doing whatever it takes to win.

Off the ice, discipline means knowing what it takes to be ready to play. You have to get the proper rest. You can't be out carousing all the time. You have to know that eventually it will catch up to you. Sure, you can go out and play with guilt for one night. I know I did. So I tell them to learn from my mistakes—do as I say, not as I did.

You might have missed curfew, or had the one more you didn't need to have, so you didn't get the proper rest or do the things conducive to being ready to play and win. So you work a little harder, you play with guilt. That can work for one night, but not as a regular routine. It has been proven time and again that the guys who are most ready are the guys who will win.

I'll never forget going down to watch the Detroit Red Wings in Montreal. Like I said earlier, I always loved Gordie Howe. To me, there was no one else in the world of hockey except Gordie Howe. Before I knew him, I'd go down to Montreal to see Detroit play, and I'll never forget after a game we happened to be in a restaurant they came into. There was Gordie and a bunch of them. They sat, ordered their meal quickly, ate and left, and went back to the hotel. This is Saturday night in Montreal. There was all sorts of trouble they could have found if they went looking. But they didn't. Discipline.

That's why a lot of them became stars and won Cups. You ask Bobby Orr about the preparation of being ready to be your best. You can have all the talent in the world, but you HAVE to be disciplined.

To get this across to my players, I'll tell stories about guys like Gordie Howe.

Gordie wanted to be the best. He would always get his proper rest and come to the rink ready. Eating at the right time, getting the proper food. In our day, we weren't given a lot of meal money. Some guys would eat at White Tower the day of the game. They had a chain in the States, beans and burgers. I was brought up to believe the proper pre-game meal was steak and baked potato. I had to have a steak. That's been proven wrong now. Now it's all pasta—quick energy.

But if you have games two nights in a row, I still say steak on a Thursday is good for Friday's game, and pasta on Friday is good for Saturday. My mother always told me, never shortchange your body of food.

In our days back in Springfield with Eddie Shore, he'd give us $4 for a day. Shore always said you could get breakfast for $1 and lunch for $1, then you'd have an extra 50 cents for dinner! There were a lot of places where you could get 99-cent breakfasts, but you'd never have any money left for dinner. Shore felt we made enough money, we could buy our own dinners. With the 67's, we made sure the kids always got enough food in their bodies.

Another rule is, you better be polite. When our team goes into a restaurant, it's hats off and it's "please" and "thank you," "yes, sir" and "no, sir." There is no fun at the table, no throwing food. Proper etiquette is important. I'd always sit where I could see all of them to make sure they were polite and courteous to the girls serving them. And if it was a buffet, I'd say, "Fellas, they don't mind if you take two or three plates. What bothers them is if you take a big plate and then don't eat it. So take just enough, and you can always go back for more. And when we leave, you always thank the servers, the chef and, if possible, the owner.

Logan Couture (Ottawa 67's forward, 2005–09): *The biggest thing I learned from him is respect. You could not leave the restaurant until you thanked every single server. It's something I still try to do.*

Seamus Kotyk (Ottawa 67's goalie, 1997–2001): *And it didn't matter where we ate, we always had to thank the chef. Sneaky Pete's Restaurant in Belleville ... KFC ... Killer always said, "Make sure you thank the cook!"*

Another thing is proper dress. I don't want someone coming in to the restaurant wearing those jeans with holes in them. I've told some guys, "If you have another pair of pants, I'd suggest you go put them on right now, or otherwise you are going to go hungry tonight." I don't make them wear a shirt and tie, because I know they pay a lot for those jeans these days. But no holes, and tuck in your shirt. And no hats! I always say to them. "Why the hat? Are you afraid the roof is going to leak?"

I'll tell the kids if they embarrass me in the hotel or restaurant, I'll show them where some of the other teams stay and eat. It's an awful lot cheaper. When we go to, say, the Bristol Place in Toronto, our pre-game meal is more than $20 per person. But we have an owner in Jeff Hunt who wants the kids to eat well. He knows it's important.

Our players know we stay in nice places and we eat in good restaurants. We have a place in Sudbury called the Caruso Club. We are one of the few teams they will allow there. Some teams didn't treat it with respect. We always did. I made sure of it.

When you get to the pros, your conduct off the ice can make a telling mark on whether you are going to make the team. If you are an ass in the dressing room, or to your trainer, or you are an ass in the restaurant, embarrassing your team, they aren't going to pick you. They are going to pick the guy who isn't the ass.

So I always look for players, and look to develop players, who are going to be respectful to other people, who are going to be men.

When a kid comes to Ottawa, he is 16. The families they stay with give them a lot. So, I tell them, when you are at home with your landladies, go out and shovel the driveway. There's a good chance there will be a chocolate cake waiting for you after. Keep your room clean, make your own bed. These are small things that matter. Respect at home, respect on the road.

I don't ever want to be called down to the front desk to hear there has been a problem in one of the players' hotel rooms. Sure, it happened a couple of times. It could be something innocent, like a pillow fight. They think it's funny, but when a pillow breaks and there are feathers all over the place for the maid to clean up, that's not funny.

I'd punish them. Maybe I'd take them out of the line up, or I'd ignore them.

One player would say, "Killer is always on me." And the smart player will respond, "You're lucky. It's when he's not on you that you're in trouble."

And that's the truth. If I've been on you, and you don't find a way to help yourself and change, and I stop getting on you, you are in trouble. Because there's a good chance you could be headed out of town.

I wanted to give my players the chance to have a life in hockey. But if they didn't get that chance, I wanted them to be ready for the real world, whatever it had in store for them.

I'll never forget Steve Payne's last game with the team (1978). In his final season, we lost out in the playoffs in Peterborough. One of our guys came in and said, "Steve's Dad wants to see you." So I went out and he said, "I just wanted to thank you. I gave you a boy and you are giving me back a man."

That meant everything to me.

14

Did I Tell You the One About ...?

JD: *Not all of Killer's tales fit into neat, tidy chapters. In fact, his best stories usually come when you simply say, "Hey, Killer, what was that guy like? Do you have any good ones about him?"*

He usually does.

The one about Terry Sawchuk faking an injury...

During my only full season in the NHL with the Los Angeles Kings, we were playing a game against Chicago. They were great back then, with Stan Mikita and Bobby Hull and all those guys. We were up by a goal late and the face-off was in our end. Well, I considered myself good on the face-offs, and so did our coach, Red Kelly. But I had just finished a shift and come off.

All of a sudden, Terry Sawchuk, our goalie, skates to the bench. He's rubbing his shoulder as if it's really hurt. He skates up to the bench, and Red comes over to see what's wrong, and Terry says, "Put Killer out for the face-off." Red says, "He just came off the ice!" Terry goes, "He's all right, put him out there." He wasn't hurt at all, he just wanted Red to know he wanted me to take that draw.

And Red listened. He put me back out there. It was me against Mikita. Now, Mikita is telling his guys exactly where to stand, he's setting them up, and that gets me even more fired up, because he figures he's going to win it. So, I set up our defence, too. The puck drops and bang! I win the draw. It rings along the boards, and Lowell MacDonald tips it out of our end. I end up picking it up and passing to Teddy Irvine. Teddy scores and we win 5-3. I ended up with a goal and an assist. I didn't have a lot of memorable games in the National League, but that was one.

I loved Terry Sawchuk. People always argue about who was the best goalie ever. Was it Glenn Hall, or Jacques Plante, or Roy or Brodeur? For me, it was Terry Sawchuk, because I saw him up close. And he was unbelievable.

The one about Mike Peca playing the whole period ...

One time, Mike was about 20 minutes late for curfew. I told him he was going to miss the next game. But I was kidding.

I wasn't a huge curfew guy, as long as you came to the rink ready to play. I'd forgotten about it by Saturday, when we were playing. So, I walk into the rink and Peca isn't getting dressed. I asked the trainer what was going on. He said, "Peca said you told him he wasn't playing." Well, we didn't have a very good team that year and Mike was our best player, so he was definitely playing.

We were playing Sault Ste. Marie and they had a strong team. But they started matching lines, and putting their checking line on Peca. They were trying to shadow him. I figured I might as well keep their best lines off the ice, so at the start of the third period, I told Mike, "You aren't coming off. No matter what happens, stay out there." I told the goalie to freeze the puck whenever he could to give Mike a breather. So, Peca never left the ice the entire period! Not once! We still lost, 3-1. But trust me, it would have been about 8-1. I loved Peca.

The one about Bill Sweeney's great escapes ...

Back when I was with Eddie Shore in Springfield, we were in Cleveland, and we had a 9 p.m. curfew. It was always a great challenge to find a way to get out of the hotel, and then sneak back in, without getting caught. Bill Sweeney was the best at it. He was like Houdini—an escape artist. So our coach, Pat Egan, issues a warning (but to us it was a challenge): "There's no way out of this hotel except the front door. Everything else is locked, and I am going to be sitting in the lobby all night, so don't even think about trying to go out."

Well, he underestimated Bill Sweeney. Bill went down to the basement, went through some underground pipes, found an iron-wrung ladder that led to a manhole, and he climbed out the manhole onto the street!

He never caused any trouble. He just wanted to sit and have a beer or two somewhere. But the next day, he couldn't stop himself. He tells Egan! He says, "I beat you last night, Eaggy boy!" Pat says, "What are you talking about Bill? I sat in the lobby bar until it closed watching the door. Nobody got out." "Well, I did," Bill says.

Another time, in Buffalo, we were all trying to get out. Most of us snuck out a back door, and went through an alley. But as we crossed the street, we saw Egan, so we ducked into another dark alleyway to wait until he was gone. Now, Egan is on the prowl for us, looking up and down the street. Then, all of a sudden, these iron grates open up on the sidewalk, and this platform rises out of it. You know, those things like they have in New York for garbage disposal or whatnot. So this thing rises out from under the sidewalk, and standing on it ... Bill Sweeney! But this time Egan is right there watching it. Sweeney got caught, and we all got away. But I'll never forget him rising out of the ground. It was like some movie scene.

One time, Bill was trying to open the outside door of his second-floor flat, pulling really hard, and he flew backwards,

A typical pose behind the bench, May 16, 1984.

Brian coaching on the ice, 1989.

1984 NEW YORK ISLANDERS 1985

Front Row: (left to right) Bill Smith, Butch Goring, Denis Potvin, Al Arbour, John O. Pickett, Jr., Bill Torrey, Brian Kilrea, Kelly Hrudey, Roland Melanson.
Second Row: Roger Kortko, Gord Lane, Duane Sutter, Dave Langevin, Clark Gillies, Bob Bourne, Stefan Persson, Bob Nystrom, Ken Morrow.
Third Row: Steve Coraci, Pat Flatley, Mats Hallin, Mike Bossy, Bryan Trottier, John Tonelli, Brent Sutter, Craig Smith, Jim Pickard.
Back Row: Pat LaFontaine, Tomas Jonsson, Paul Boutilier, Gerald Diduck, Greg Gilbert, Gord Dineen, Anders Kallur.

Brian, third from the right, front row, was assistant coach with the Islanders for two seasons before returning to the 67's for the rest of his coaching career.

Memorial Cup champs, 1999. Brian is on the far right, with assistant coach, Bert O'Brien, kneeling below him. This was Brian's second Memorial Cup win with the 67's, after first capturing the Cup in 1984. To the left of Brian in the white t-shirt is 67's owner Jeff Hunt. Lance Galbraith (of chapter 5, "A Chance on Lance") is #71, laughing in the back row. Also on this championship team were Nick Boynton and Brian Campbell, who both made it to the NHL and won the Stanley Cup with the Chicago Blackhawks in 2010.

OHL Commissioner David Branch presenting Brian with the OHL Milestone Award for 500 wins in 1989. Kilrea would go on to hit 1,193 wins in his coaching career—more than any other coach in junior hockey history.

Brian with best friend and longtime assistant Bert O'Brien (left), and longtime friend and Kingston Frontenacs GM Larry Mavety, after Brian's final regular season game, the last of his record 1,193 wins.

Killer behind the bench in his final season, 2008-09.

A tearful, but clearly tickled, Brian, right after getting the phone call that he was going to be inducted into the Hockey Hall of Fame, June 26, 2003. By the way, that is not Killer's cell phone. He has never had one. And never will.

With other HHOF inductees at the ceremony, November 3, 2003. From left, Mike Ilitch (Detroit Red Wings owner), Pat Lafontaine, Grant Fuhr.

With Don Cherry at Brian's retirement ceremony.

The perfect head cover! Likely to get lots of use in Brian's life after coaching.

Brian and Bobby Orr.

Brian and buddy Don Cherry.

right over the railing! He was really lucky he didn't break anything, but he was pretty banged up. His shoulder and leg were
badly bruised. So he comes to the rink on the day of a game,
and Shore says, "Get dressed. I wanna see if you can play."
Bill goes out there, Shore throws some pucks on the ice and
says, "Let me see you stickhandle." Bill couldn't stickhandle.
"Let me see you shoot." Bill couldn't shoot. Shore says, "Get
off the ice! You're suspended for indifferent play!" Indifferent
play, for falling off his balcony!

Bill comes back in the room and shrugs, "Suspended
again, guys."

The one about making love to a buffalo ...

We were playing Oshawa in the playoffs, and they took the
first three games against us. So it's Game 4, and they are beating us 3-2 in the last minute. We call a time-out, and the guys
come over to the bench. Now, there is this one guy in the
crowd who has been yelling at us the whole night, taunting
our guys. He's only about six rows behind our bench. So I say
to the kids, "You see that guy up there, the one with the red
hair and the moustache and beard? I have to confess something to you guys. About 20 years ago, I made love to a buffalo.
That guy might be my son."

Well, the kids start laughing. I have a few seconds left in
the time-out, so I get serious and tell them to win the face-off
and get to the net. Sure enough, the puck eventually goes in
front of their net, it goes off their own guy, and in. We tie the

game with 21 seconds left. We win in overtime, we win the next three games and take the series. We become the first team in the league ever to come back from 0-3!

The one about Andrew Cassels and the shampoo ...

Andrew was a great kid, but he could be a shit-disturber. He had this sweet, innocent face. If he did something wrong, he's give you this "Who me?" look. But he was usually guilty. Well, I used to always take a shower in the dressing room after practice, just like the players. So one day we're practising at Canterbury Arena. They had this brick half-wall around the shower area, and Andrew climbed up and went right above where I was showering. I was washing my hair, and as I was rinsing it out, he kept pouring more shampoo on my head. I couldn't open my eyes, and I couldn't figure out why it was taking so long to get my hair rinsed. This went on for five minutes. I was yelling and getting more and more upset, and he just kept pouring more shampoo on me. The players were breaking up. I think I said, "I'm going to trade whoever did this to me!" But there was no chance I was trading Andrew Cassels. He was a character, but, boy, could he play hockey. He is still the only player ever to be voted team MVP all three years he was with the 67's.

The one about Gerry Foley and the stolen sandwiches ...

Gerry Foley was one of the best guys I ever met. I played with him for years in Springfield. But we got him good one night.

He came up with this brilliant idea to make a buck. We were on the road, and he knew the guys would be hungry on the bus after the game. So, he goes over to the store before the game and buys bread and butter and lettuce and cold cuts, and makes a bunch of sandwiches. He was selling them for two or three bucks—a lot for a sandwich back then. A couple of guys bought them, but most didn't.

So Gerry eats a couple himself, then says to Jimmy Wilcox, "Watch my sandwiches. I'm gonna have a nap." But Wilcox fell asleep, too.

Well, put it this way, we might have had a couple of pops, and when Gerry woke up, the sandwiches were gone and so was the money. Gerry says, "Wilcox, wake up! Did you sell all my sandwiches?" Jimmy says, "No." Then Gerry just went off. "Who took my sandwiches?!?" Where's my money?!?" It was hilarious.

The one about Peter Lee never leaving practice ...

I have never seen a player train and practise as hard as Peter Lee. He was always the hardest worker on the ice. Every drill, he would do full out. He would never slow down three feet from the line on a skating drill. He always finished it. In those days, I would practise about an hour and 45 minutes, so we'd get off the ice around a quarter to six. But Peter wouldn't come off. I'd go into the room, talk to the players, have a shower, dress, do some work. It would be 6:45 and Peter Lee was still on the ice!

He tried everything to get better. He would glue two pucks together to strengthen his shot. But they kept splitting, so we had to buy him those rusty red weighted pucks. He would fire them for hours. He was the first one on the ice, and he wouldn't get off until after 7:00. The trainers were getting mad at him. They wanted to lock up and leave, but they were always waiting for Peter.

And it paid off. He was a helluva player. Scored 81 goals his last year. And there was no such thing as a road game for Peter. The tougher the rink, the better he played. He never slowed down in the corners. I could have played him 30 minutes a game, and it wouldn't have been enough.

It bothers me when people say they thought Peter should have been a much better player in the National League. The guy scored more than 30 goals twice. He left over a contract thing and went to Europe. Peter Lee was a great player. One of the best I ever had.

The one about drinking the Cleveland Barons under the table . . .

Back in my playing days, there were nights you would run into the other team at the bar. One night, we were out with a bunch of guys from the Cleveland Barons, and I was talking with Bobby Ellett about which guys were real stayers at the bar—who could handle their beer the best. So, we made a bet. We were each allowed to pick five guys from our team. The rule was if one guy ordered a beer, everyone drank one. Well, within an hour or two, Bobby's guys had three or four beers each lined up on the table, and my team's glasses were all empty. In fact, our guys decided to have a shot with each beer, and it still didn't matter. Bobby and his guys couldn't believe it. We destroyed them. And then we did the same thing to them on the ice. As we're skating off, I said to Bobby, "The team that drinks together wins together!"

We just had one of those teams. A bunch of real characters who loved to have a good time, but some great players.

The one about Tim Young's sore thigh ...

Tim Young was a really gifted offensive player, but he didn't like pain. One time, he told me he had a charley horse, so I brought him up to the front of the bus and sat him next to me. I did what Eddie Shore used to do to me. I said, "Tim, sit still. I'll work it out." So I put my thumbs on the spot that hurt, and I started pressing and rubbing. I started getting deeper and deeper into his thigh, and his ass started coming out of the seat. So I kept on pushing, and he started yelling in agony. He was right off the seat, just screaming! But he played the next day, so the remedy worked. Either that, or he was scared about coming back for another session. Tim almost won the scoring title that year. He was ahead of a guy named Mike Kaszycki, who played for Sault Ste. Marie. But with only a couple of games left, Kaszycki gets 11 points in one game! I think that hurt Tim more than my massage.

The one about Jimmy Anderson's shoes (and suit) . . .

One of the great practical jokes in hockey is when they nail a guy's shoes to the floor. They did it to Jimmy Anderson in Springfield. Put a nail through each sole, and put socks on top of the nails. So when Jimmy gets up and tries to walk . . . it doesn't go so well!

Jimmy was a well-liked guy who pulled his share of pranks, so guys had to get even. One time, Jimmy had this really nice suit on. So they cut off the legs of his pants, and cut the sleeves out of his jacket. Jimmy had no other clothes to put on, so he had to wear the suit. Eddie Shore comes in and yells at Jimmy: "That's no way to dress in winter!"

I can't remember who did it to him, but I do remember that Jimmy didn't squeal on the guy. He just left, and boy, did he ever look funny leaving the rink with those short pants and no sleeves.

The one about Grant Marshall and Eric Lindros . . .

One of the scariest moments in my coaching career was the night Grant Marshall broke his neck. We were in Sudbury and I wasn't even on the bench. I was suspended, so I was sitting in the stands. Grant got run from behind and hit the boards. He told the trainer he was OK, and got to the bench by himself, but then he was in discomfort, and they had to get the stretcher.

At first they wouldn't let me see him at the hospital.
There's not much worse for a coach than knowing one of
your players has been seriously hurt. You have told their parents you will take care of them. You feel responsible. We
weren't sure about his hockey future. He was in a halo for
two months. He would come to practice every day and stand
by the boards. Some of those rinks were so cold, you could
see the frost forming on those pegs in his forehead. But then
he started skating, and before long he wanted to play again.

Now we're in the semi-finals against Eric Lindros and
Oshawa. Between Games 6 and 7, Grant goes to his doctor in
Toronto and gets clearance to play. But I'm nervous. I would
rather he put it off, take the summer to make sure he's OK.
So I say, "You need a letter from your parents." Sure enough,
he gets a letter from his Mom and Dad, saying he has their
permission to play.

I agree to put him in the line up, but I really have no intention of playing him, except maybe a couple of shifts. So I put
him out there, and immediately, he takes a run at Eric Lindros!
When he gets back to the bench I say, "Grant, what are you
doing?!?" He goes, "I want Lindros to know I'm all right."

I don't think I've ever seen determination like Grant
Marshall showed that year.

I also respected what Lindros did. He could have run
Grant over. But he backed off.

I loved Lindros. I hear people say things about him now,
and it bothers me. He was a gentleman, and a real asset to
our league. He did a lot of stuff behind the scenes people

didn't know about. I was involved with the Children's Hospital, and he would always sign things for me. His brother, Brett, was the same way. They were class guys.

The one about Gordie Hamilton's laughing fit ...

Gordie was my cousin, and he used to be my assistant coach. We had these two brothers, Kent Brimmer and Chuck Brimmer. Kent was a centreman, Chuck was a defenceman. Anyway, we were in Oshawa and Chuck was carrying the puck over the blue line and turning towards centre when he just got steamrolled. He was down and out. He was really groggy. But I give him credit, he was able to get up and stumble over to the boards near our bench. The bench was quiet. Everybody was concerned. So I went down to have a look, and once I knew he wasn't badly hurt, I said, "Atta boy, Chuck! That's the way to hit 'em! Let's all be more physical like Chuck!" I just deadpanned it. Gordie looked at me, and he started to crack up.

He started laughing so hard, he had to leave the bench. He was down in the hallway by the dressing room. My trainer went to check on him. He came back and said, "Gordie will come back to the bench, but only if you promise not to say another word."

The one about Sean Simpson practising in a suit ...

Simmer was born in England, and I figured he had a chance to go to the World Juniors. That was when the Memorial

Cup champ would go, but they could pick up a few players from other teams. Peterborough was the team going, and Simmer played with Jimmy Fox and Yvan Joly, so I figured the whole line might get picked up. I wanted to make sure Simmer had his passport so he could go to Europe if they picked him. Of course, he didn't.

So Simmer goes through the whole process and gets his Canadian citizenship. Well, on the day he gets it, he comes straight from the ceremony to practice. He comes on the ice wearing a helmet, shin pads and his full suit and tie! And he's taken black tape and put his "A" on the front of his suit.

We all laughed. He stayed out for a couple of drills, then went and got his gear on. That was Simmer, one of a kind.

I just couldn't get rid of him. He had left junior and was playing in Europe, but he came back for that Memorial Cup in Kitchener that we won. He shows up on the Tuesday and says, "I just want you to know I'm here to support you." So I say. "Okay, Sim. I'll get you tickets." He says, "Well, I need somewhere to sleep, too." So I say, "Okay, Sim, you can stay in my son Billy's room for the night. How long are you staying?" "Till it's over, Coach!"

Well, every day I would see him in the corridor and say, "How?"

"How what?"

"How *!#&'ing long are you here?"

Then later in the day I'd see him and say, "When?"

"When what?"

"When are you &#!*'ing leaving?"

Well, he never left. We get on the bus after we win, and everyone is celebrating, and one of the guys yells, "Look, Simmer is with a girl!" Everyone looks out and Sim is up against a tree with his back to us, and it looks like he's making out with some girl. Then he turns around, and it was just his own arms.

JD: *I believe this technique was first perfected by Ralph Malph on* Happy Days.

Everyone was laughing so hard, for a minute we forgot we won the Memorial Cup. That was Sean Simpson.

Another time, Jimmy Fox was doing an All-Ugly Team for the league. Well, he went through a few of the positions. And he got to centre and he said, "Sim, you're the centre." Sim was baffled. "I'm on it?" So he came to me and said, "Coach, Fox is picking an All-Ugly Team and he says I'm on it. What do you think?"

I waited a couple of seconds and said, "Good pick."

The one about Dale Rolfe's disguise . . .

Dale was tough, on the ice and off. One time, in Philadelphia, while we were playing for the Los Angeles Kings, some guy was jawing with Terry Sawchuk outside a bar, so Dale sees this and goes boom! Pops him, knocks him out. The next morning we're getting ready to get on the bus and the cops show up. They don't know Dale's name, but they know they're looking for a tall guy with a big nose who plays on our team.

Well, Artie Stratton used to wear glasses that were coke bottles. So, I take Artie's glasses, and we grab somebody else's hat, and put them on Dale Rolfe. We sneak him out in disguise and put him in a cab.

Cops couldn't seem to find the guy they were looking for on the bus!

The one about cowboy Timmy Higgins and his horse Bobby Smith ...

There aren't too many funny stories about Bobby Smith because he was so focused, so serious, so dedicated to getting better. I consider myself a pretty good face-off man, and when I'd beat him in practice, he would stay there, wanting to do more and more until he beat me. And as he got bigger and stronger, he started beating me.

Anyway, Bobby hated exhibition games. We had a weekend off, and I had a friend in Rochester with a Tier 2 team that wanted to play us. Bobby didn't want to go at all. But we went, and he had fun. In fact, at one point during the game, Bobby was cutting across the ice, and Timmy Higgins was cutting across, and somehow they both fell and Timmy ended up on Bobby's back. Well, they are sliding past our bench, and Timmy puts his arm in the air like he's riding a buckin' bronco! Then Bobby looks up and he's smiling and he waves to the bench. Right in the middle of the game, and these guys are in their own rodeo.

I remember Bobby coming to me after and saying, "That was fun. I'm glad I came."

The one about Dick Hunter and the bikers . . .

Dick Hunter was one of the toughest guys I ever met. You could see where his boys Dale and Mark got it from. One night, we were in a bar in Kitchener, sitting at a table next to all these bikers. Well, one of the biker's girlfriends gets up to light her cigarette, and Dick pulls her chair away. He didn't do it on purpose. He needed a chair for someone, and didn't notice this girl was about to sit back down on it. So she sits back and falls right on her behind. I'm thinking, "We're in big trouble now." But Dick doesn't apologize or anything, he just says to the girl, "What the hell are you doing down there?" I still don't know how we made it out of there alive.

The one about Gordie Wood and the fish hook . . .

Gordie Wood was one of the greatest characters you'll ever meet. He was the head scout for the Cornwall Royals when they won two Memorial Cups. He found Dale Hawerchuk. Later, he'd come work with the 67's and help us win our second Memorial Cup.

But Gordie was an accident waiting to happen. He would leave the house looking immaculate. He always wore a beautiful fedora, like Punch Imlach. He'd have on a suit and tie. He'd look like he just walked out of *Esquire*. But by the first intermission of whatever game he was at, he'd be a mess! There would be mustard on his coat, his tie would be off, and his hair would be all over the place because he kept taking off his hat, he'd get so excited.

Back when Gordie was a ballplayer—and he was a good one—he hit a line drive that went between the outfielders. By the time he rounded first, one sock was down. By second base, the other sock was down. And by the time he rounded third, his pants were down around his ankles! Gordie was a mess.

One time, he takes his wife Thelma's brother fishing. Now this guy was really anxious to get the hook in the water. Gordie kept saying, "Wait till we get out in deeper water and I throw out the anchor." So, they get out there, and just as Gordie is tossing the anchor, he turns around and the guy is throwing his hook in the water. It catches Gordie right on his mouth! He hooked him through his lip! Gordie could swear with the best of them when he was mad and he let loose with a barrage. He goes to the hospital in Kingston, and he hasn't cut off the spoon. He walks into Emergency, and he has the spoon in one hand and the hook through his lip, and the nurse says, "Can I help you?" Gordie goes, "No! I always walk around with one of these things in my lip!"

The doctor comes in and says, "We can fix that." He gets a pair of snips, and Gordie says, "You're not going to pull that thing out, are ya?!?" He thinks the doc is going to treat him like a bass! "Relax, Gord," says the doctor, and he cuts the hook and slides it out. That's one of my all-time favorites.

I loved getting Gordie worked up. When he was with Cornwall, and we were rivals, I saw him at a Tier 2 game up in Pembroke that I was scouting. He was lying low, almost hiding behind a pillar. I come up and say, "Hey, Gordie." He says, "What are you doing here?" I say, "Well, I called your son Barry, and he told me this was the game you were coming to. So I figured I better get up here. This must be the game to see." Of course, I'd made that up. I was coming to the game all along. Anyway, Barry calls me the next week and says, "Will you please tell my Dad I didn't tell you he was going to that game. He won't talk to me because he thinks I tipped you off!"

We shared laughs right till the end. When his health was failing, and he knew he didn't have long, he called and said, "I'd like you and Don Cherry to say a few words at my funeral." I said, "You mean, do the eulogy? Well, if you want me to drive all the way to Kingston on my own gas, you better leave me something in your will!" He laughed.

Of course, when Gordie passed, Don and I were there to speak. Gordie was one of the greats. And one of the great friends of my life.

The one about Doug Wilson's double-or-nothing bet . . .

We were on the road in Niagara Falls, and Dougie Wilson and his roommate Larry Skinner came in about 20 minutes after curfew. I had put a note on their door: "Come see me before you go to bed." So they come in, and I say, "Doug, I'm going to have to fine you. And, Larry, you're not going to be in the line up anyway, so I'm sending you home."

Dougie comes back a few minutes later and says, "I'll make a deal with you. I'll go double or nothing on the game. If we win, I don't pay the fine. And one other thing, you can't send Skinner home tomorrow."

So I agree. And what does Dougie do? He goes out and scores two goals, a couple of assists, and we win the game.

And to top it off, he squares off with this real tough guy they had on their team near the end of the game. Dougie beat the crap out of him. As he's skating past the bench to the box, he says, "There's no fine."

The one about my first game in Los Angeles ...

After my years in Springfield with Eddie Shore, I went to Los Angeles when the NHL expanded. We were losing 2-0 to Philadelphia, when the puck came to me in the slot. I took a quick wrist shot, it found a hole and went in. It was my first goal in the National League, and the first goal ever for the Los Angeles Kings.

I would get an assist later, and we had a 4-3 lead late in the game, with the Flyers net empty. So, Red Kelly, our coach, puts me out for a face-off in our end in the last minute. I get the puck and fire it the length of the ice. I knew right away that was a mistake because it was going to be icing.

Just as I shoot it, I get knocked down. As I am trying to get up to watch the puck, praying it somehow won't be icing, Dale Rolfe, who is standing behind me, says, "You can stay down, it's in."

So in LA's first-ever game, and my first full NHL game, the first since that one shift with Gordie Howe and Ted Lindsay eight years before, I scored two goals and an assist.

Our owner, Jack Kent Cooke, came into the room after, and was shaking everyone's hands. He came to me and I handed him the puck. I said, "Here's the first goal your team ever scored. I want you to have it." He said, "You'd give that to me?"

I said, "Sure, I don't think I'll be scoring too many goals, so it won't be worth too much!" I think he put it on a plaque. Who knows where it is now?

Jack was a super guy. He owned the Lakers, too. He invited us over to his place. It was unbelievable, like a museum of sport. We were hanging around guys like Elgin Baylor and Jerry West.

But still, I didn't like Los Angeles. It just wasn't a hockey atmosphere, and I wanted to be closer to home. Twenty-five games in, I hurt my knee and lost a stride I never had. While I was out with the injury, I went to the team and asked to get sent down to Springfield.

I know. Not many guys ask to leave the National Hockey League for the American League. But I knew the LA Kings weren't going to build a team around a 33-year-old centreman. After a while, they agreed to send me down. I'd bounce around for two more years, and then I retired.

Could I have played longer in the NHL? Who knows? I never think about it. Everything happens for a reason, and things work out for the best. I ended up back in Ottawa where I wanted to be, got into coaching, and ... well, you know the rest.

I do sometimes wonder where that puck is, though.

15

The Call of the Hall

I was a hard-working hockey player, but I knew from the outset I was never going to be a Hall-of-Famer. It was the same with coaching. I was fortunate enough to have a lot of success coaching, but it was junior, not the pros. So there was no chance I was ever going to be in the Hockey Hall of Fame. In fact, it never even entered my mind.

Then one day in 2003, I was being honored down at Ottawa City Hall. I was just mingling around, talking to some reporters, when Pat Whalen, CEO of the 67's, got a call on his cell phone and handed it to me. I didn't have a cell phone; still don't. So I guess they had been trying to reach me for a while.

It was Jim Gregory (Hockey Hall of Fame Selection Committee Co-Chair). He said, "Brian, you've been voted into the Hockey Hall of Fame."

I was stunned. It was—it is—the single greatest honour of my life.

Jim told me I couldn't tell anyone, because the official announcement wasn't going to come until 6 p.m. I said, "Uhh, I got a bit of a problem, Jim. There are a whole bunch of Ottawa press people standing right in front of me, looking at me right now." I'm sure my face was beaming. They saw how excited I was, they knew something was up. I wasn't sure what to do. But I looked around and there were no radio guys there, just some TV and print guys. So I figured the TV newscasts aren't until 6:00, and the papers aren't out until the morning, so I'd be okay. So I told them.

JD: *Apparently, Killer had temporarily forgotten that little Internet thingy.*

I was in shock. Back in my playing days, I was labelled a shit-disturber because of what happened with the strike with Eddie Shore, and then attending the union meeting in the AHL and getting sent down the next day. I was exiled, and now I was going into the Hall of Fame. I was walking on air.

I went home with a few friends because I was supposed to wait for the official call from Bill Hay (Hockey Hall of Fame Chairman). I remember wishing my Mom and Dad were there, and my three uncles who played in the NHL, because I had followed in their footsteps. They were the reason I chose a life in hockey.

Bobby Smith (Ottawa 67's forward, 1975–78): *Before I bought the Halifax Mooseheads, I was taking a look at the Portland Winterhawks. I remember being in Portland, and my cell phone rang. I can't remember who called, but they told me Killer had just been voted into the Hockey Hall of Fame. I was so excited, it made my day. I remember thinking how ridiculous it was that he wasn't already in. He had the kind of influence basketball coach John Wooden had in the U.S. Think about it. I don't think there is a guy in the Hall who influenced more young hockey players than Brian Kilrea.*

I won three Calder Cups in Springfield, coached the Ottawa 67's to two Memorial Cup titles and won Coach of the Year a few times. But there is nothing like the Hall of Fame.

I don't think I would have gotten that call without (OHL commissioner) David Branch. I think, behind the scenes, he was the one who made a big push for me to get in the Hall. I truly believe David is the most important individual ever for junior hockey in this country. He's always been one step ahead of everyone else—in terms of protecting our kids, in terms of the education programs he's put in place. The best move this league ever made was bringing in David Branch. He's been a great friend, and I owe him a lot.

I had a lot of people to thank. I didn't write my speech until the day of the induction ceremony. I knew they wanted us to limit it to a few minutes, so I didn't want to give myself too much time to write it. I just wanted to make sure I thanked all the people responsible for getting me there: my family, the assistant coaches, the players, the scouts that brought me the players.

Many of my players came for the ceremony. As I was thanking them, I could see Bobby Smith and Doug Wilson in the crowd and I almost lost it. It meant so much to me that they were there.

Doug Wilson (Ottawa 67's defenceman, 1974–77): *Killer is so humble, I remember thinking that night that he was wondering if he really even belonged there. He still doesn't realize he is one of the greatest gifts to hockey.*

The whole night was unforgettable. I was in awe of everyone and everything there. Even meeting Bill Hay, I was in awe, knowing everything he stands for. The voters are never supposed to tell you that they voted for you, but I could tell, because some of them were so happy for me.

Afterwards, Jeff Hunt rented this huge room, almost a ballroom, and brought in a portable bar. Jeff always wanted to do things right. The cost never mattered. My family, friends and former players came back. It was one of the greatest nights of my life.

Bobby Smith: *Just hanging out in that hotel after was the best part. And that was Killer. Sure, the tuxedo stuff, the ceremony, that was fabulous. But to him, it was all about having a couple of beers with these players who had come in from all over. Dougie, Jimmy Fox, we just told stories and laughed and laughed.*

I go to the ceremony every year, wearing my blazer. I was just this junior coach, but now all the NHL legends recognize me. I've been accepted by the greats of hockey, and I still can't believe that.

When Scotty Bowman, the greatest coach ever, will take 15 minutes or a half hour to sit and talk with you ... Or Gordie Howe, the greatest player ever, will chat with you ... It's the greatest club in the world to be a member of.

Brian Kilrea's Hall of Fame Induction Speech—November 3, 2003

I'd like to start by saying the last three days I've had the most enjoyable time being here with all of these inductees. I'd like to congratulate Grant Fuhr. I'd never met him before, and to come here and to be so humble and so good-natured, it's just incredible. Mr. Ilitch was just as you saw him up here, enjoyable and fun to be around. And Pat LaFontaine, when he was on time for the meetings, is a super guy to talk to. (*Laughter*) Pat would time a lot of things a little close, but he was there, and he is again, one of those priceless individuals who typified success.

I'd like to thank Bill Hay and the Hockey Hall of Fame Committee for the tremendous honour one could only dream about—to be alongside the individuals who have made the game of hockey the greatest game in the world. I'd like to thank my wife Judy, my biggest fan and supporter, who always stayed in the background while bringing up the family: my son Billy, daughters Diane and Linda, whom I am so very proud of; as well as our extended family and grandchildren.

Judy actually got me started in coaching, volunteering my name for the tyke program in Ottawa. They were short of coaches and you didn't have to have any experience. They just needed somebody to volunteer, so Judy volunteered my name and it was a couple years later that I was coaching a midget team in Ottawa, and the Ottawa 67's. Jack Kinsella and Howard Henry, Howard Darwin and Bill Cowley came and talked to me and wondered if I'd be interested in coaching the Ottawa 67's. Naturally, I said yes. I didn't realize that I should have been bartering for a salary, but I was just so happy to be coaching that I think the first year I broke even. (*Laughter*)

The next year, Earl Montagano came along and it was a wonderful association. And then in '99, Mr. Jeff Hunt took over and it's just been a very enjoyable thing. They were my bosses, but they became my best friends, and who could ever fire your best friend? So I think my job was safe because of that.

I feel very fortunate to be able to coach in the OHL under the direction of Dave Branch. Not just the improvements he's made, but where his motto has been "players first," and that's the way I feel myself. I'm fortunate to have made so many friends through my hockey years. The media, who have always been so supportive. I thank you very much.

I would like to thank my coaching staff, who don't get enough credit for what they do. The one gentleman, Bert O'Brien, who has been with me 18 years. Another fella, Vince Malette, who has only been with me eight years. And our scouting staff, headed by a fella named Joe Rowley, who's been with me only 20 years. They have continuously provided the Ottawa 67's with such tremendous talent. And to all of the players who have contributed to the success we have enjoyed, and the friendships we have made; you are the reason I am here today.

I never thought, when I started a long time ago, that I would still be connected with hockey, but as my Dad always said, things always work out for the best. And there is nothing better than this.

Thank you.

16

Winger for Life

The injury that changed my life, for the better, happened when I was 23. I was playing with the Edmonton Flyers in the Red Wings organization. Kent Douglas hit me real hard and hurt my shoulder. It didn't pop out, but I couldn't move.

It was near the end of the season, and our coach, Bud Poile, knew it looked bad. So Bud said, "You might as well go home to Ottawa." My season was over.

Our team was playing in Winnipeg the night I was flying home. Before I got hurt, I was planning on seeing my good friend Bill Tibbs there. Turns out my flight back to Ottawa happened to have a stopover in Winnipeg, so I asked the stewardess if I could get off the plane to call Bill, just to tell him I wouldn't get to see him because I was on my way home. She let me off the plane, and I called Bill. "That's too bad," he said. "My girlfriend Doris has a friend named Judy who we were going to bring with us to the game. We thought we could all go out together after."

I must admit, that got my interest a little. Bill said, "Why don't you stay here, anyway? You can stay at Debra and George's place." (Bill's sister and her husband)

I figured, "Why not?" So I got my bag off the plane, Bill picked me up, and the four of us ended up going to the game together: Bill, his girlfriend Doris, her friend Judy and me.

I'm still not sure how this kind of thing works. Maybe lightning just strikes you. Who knows? But from the first second I met Judy, we got along great. Was it love at first sight? You better ask her.

Judy Kilrea: *I remember Doris and Bill picking me up to go to the game, and seeing this young man sitting in the back of the car. I was totally surprised he was there. I didn't really know anything about him. I don't think it was love at first sight or anything like that. I just thought he was a nice fella.*

All I know is that I was only supposed to stay that one night, but I decided to stick around for a couple more days. And even when I had to go back to Ottawa to get my shoulder looked at, I knew I wanted to come back to Winnipeg. Fast.

As luck would have it, Bill and Doris were getting married that summer, so I drove out for the wedding. Judy was one of the bridesmaids. I stayed for a week while they went on their honeymoon.

By the time they got back, Judy and I were engaged.

And to think some questioned my speed!

Judy: *He didn't get down on one knee or anything fancy like that. He just asked me. And I thought it sounded like a pretty good idea!*

We got along great. That week, I'd go to her work and take her out for lunch every day. Then we'd see each other again in the evening, go to movies. I met her family and, well, sometimes you just know. And I knew.

I had never had a serious girlfriend before. I thought the whole world revolved around hockey, until I met her.

I remember talking to her father and he wanted to know when we were planning on getting married. We told him we were thinking of July. Well, this was June! I think he was a little shocked. He said, "Maybe you might want to wait until next year." But Judy told him, "I'm not going to get to know Brian any better in the next year if he's playing hockey in Troy, Iowa." (That's where I was headed, to play for Detroit's International League team.)

So we were married July 19, 1958, about a month after Bill and Doris's wedding, and three months after we first met.

Judy: *We arranged the whole wedding through the mail. Brian was back in Ottawa, so we wrote letters every day to each other.*

The mailman delivered even on Sundays back then. Brian arrived back in Winnipeg on a Wednesday, we had the rehearsal and we got married on Saturday.

Our honeymoon consisted of driving through various states in the U.S., seeing different places. We ended up in Detroit, staying at my Uncle Hec's cottage in Bell River. It was this great spot on an inlet. I'd sit and listen to baseball games and Judy would swim. It was a wonderful time.

Fifty-two years later, we're still together. Those quicky engagements just never work! Like I keep saying, everything happens for a reason, and things always work out for the best. Kent Douglas hit me that night in Edmonton, and I ended up meeting Judy and getting to spend all that time with her because I was hurt.

Judy came down to live with me in Troy the next season. Before long, she was pregnant. The next spring, we were back in Ottawa watching a Stanley Cup Final game when her water broke. I'll never forget. It was Detroit vs. Montreal. My Mom said, "You better get her to the hospital."

I said, "Maybe we can wait until the intermission."

Now, remember in those days, you brought your wife to the hospital and left. The doctor would call you when she had the baby. So, I went home and watched the hockey game. That was the game when Tony Leswick took the shot that went off Doug Harvey's glove and into the net. Detroit won the cup. They were my team, too.

Then the doctor called and said I had a baby boy. So, I saw Leswick score the goal, and Billy Kilrea came into the world. All in all, a pretty perfect night!

We'd have two more kids, both beautiful girls: Linda and Diane. I've been blessed with a wonderful family.

I couldn't have chosen a better partner than Judy for the life I've had. She came with me wherever hockey took me. The only time she stayed back in Ottawa was my last year in hockey when I had a spinal fusion and didn't play the first half of the season. I went out and finished the year in Denver, and Judy stayed back with the kids.

Judy: *I didn't really know what I was getting into when I married Brian. I didn't know anybody who had married a hockey player. I didn't know I would be packing and unpacking, moving over and over again every year. We would start the kids in school in September in Ottawa, while Brian was in training camp, wherever it was. Then we'd rent the house out, and pack up this little two-wheeled trailer we had. We'd just take dishes and toys and clothes, and I'd line the car with our blankets and pillows and sheets so we wouldn't have to buy new stuff. Off we'd go, to wherever Brian was playing that year. When I think back, I say, "Oh my God! How did I ever do this!" But you never thought about it back then. It was just our life. And I enjoyed it.*

Judy always supported every move I made. When I started coaching, she always said, "Don't worry about me and the kids. If you want to go somewhere, we'll go."

And there were a few offers. We did spend those two years on Long Island, but when I coached the 67's, I just felt right at home. I was coaching in my hometown, my kids never had to move. Ottawa was always going to be our home, even if we did decide to go coach somewhere else; we were always coming back to Ottawa eventually.

I can't remember Judy ever getting very mad at me. Wait, there was this one time when we were living in Springfield. We had Noel Price and his wife Joanne over for dinner. He was playing for the Baltimore Clippers, and we were playing them the next night. So Judy makes this beautiful stew, but Noel says he can't eat meat because it's Friday. In those days, a lot of Catholics wouldn't eat meat on Fridays. So, I took Noel out to get some eggs for dinner.

Let's just say Judy wasn't too pleased about us leaving.

But one night in the doghouse isn't bad for more than 50 years together!

Judy never interfered with my coaching, except for one time when she got on me for a trade I almost made.

This was the mid-70s and our team was really struggling. One of our players, Jimmy Roberts, not the one from Montreal with the big cigar, another Jimmy Roberts, had been in a real slump. I made a deal with Bert Templeton, who was coaching the Hamilton Fincups. I was going to trade Jimmy, and I was going to get Joe Kowal back. But before the deal was done, I went to Peter Lee, our best player, and talked to him. Peter said, "Jimmy didn't want you to know, but his mother has been diagnosed with breast cancer."

Wow, was I glad he told me that. It explained a lot. I went right to Jimmy and said, "You go home and be with your Mom, and when she's feeling better, you come back. Don't ever worry about your place on this team." So he did, and when he came back, he had the best second half of any left winger in the league.

But I remember going home that night I found out about his Mom, and I told Judy and Billy I had almost traded Jimmy Roberts.

Judy said, "It's a good thing you didn't make that trade. He's a great guy."

"Best guy in the room," my son Billy added. I was the bad guy in my house for even thinking about trading Jimmy.

Judy: *Jimmy was my favorite. He was a really likeable young man. And it wasn't only Billy and I who were mad at Brian for thinking about trading him. Brian's Mom was living with us at the time. She used to listen to all the games on the radio. She got mad at him, too!*

That's the only time Judy ever questioned my coaching decisions.

Judy: *That's because if he was thinking about doing something, he didn't tell us about it anymore. I guess he learned his lesson with Jimmy!*

My son Billy was more involved because he knew the players. He was a pretty good player himself, and he used to practise with us and go out with the players after. I was really tough on him. I'd pick on him during practice, because I knew the players would gravitate towards him. He got to know a lot of them really well.

Billy never got a chance to play growing up when I was playing in Springfield because none of the other players brought their kids to the rink, so he was behind by the time we got back to Ottawa. He wasn't a great skater, but he had great hands, a good shot and a great head.

One year, Billy was trying to move up from midget to junior B, trying out for the team I used to coach—I'd given it to Bert O'Brien. Bert was really trying hard to keep him, so I went to him and said, "I'll save you a cut. Billy's not making it. I'll tell him." So, I told Billy he wasn't going to make it, but I'd already talked to a midget B team and he had a spot there. He was okay with it, and he made Bert's team the next year.

Billy still plays hockey on Thursday nights. He's had his own bailiff business for the last decade or so in Ottawa. He's done well. He has three boys: Dan, Dave and Jack.

My daughter Diane is in customs. She used to work with the drug squad in the RCMP, but she married a customs officer and got into that field. They're up in Yellowknife now. They have two kids, Morgan and Paige.

Our other daughter, Linda, is a nurse. She and her husband also have two children, Ben and Katie.

And no, I'm not pushing any of the grandkids into hockey. Whatever they choose to do, it's fine by me.

A great wife, three wonderful kids and seven beautiful grandchildren. All because Kent Douglas hurt my shoulder that night in Edmonton.

Thanks, Kent. I owe ya.

17

Eyewitness to a Killer

JD: *As you've seen, Killer has a library of stories about the people he has coached and played with over his life in hockey. Well, seems they have plenty about him, too. Here are some eyewitness accounts of life with Brian Kilrea.*

STEVE PAYNE (Ottawa 67's forward, 1976–78)
One night in London, Tim Higgins and Steve Marengere were up to no good. They were Frick and Frack, those two. They were always playing practical jokes. So they call me to their room. I knock, Higgins opens the door, and Marengere blasts me with a full bucket of water. They are laughing their asses off. Meanwhile, I'm drenched, and I'm pissed.

Bobby Smith and I immediately start plotting revenge. We fill up a bucket and wait inside the room for them. This is a hotel where the rooms open up to outside, like a motel. I am peeking out the drapes, and we can see them outside. There's a knock on the door. Bobby opens it, and I launch the bucket right away. As the water is flying, I realize it's Killer! It hits him square on. Completely soaks him. He was livid. He pulled me aside later and said, "You're lucky you are on a line with Bobby Smith."

Killer called me Rags. He is still the only person in the world who calls me Rags. I was pretty intense and kind of crabby back in junior, so sometimes the guys would say, "Payne is on the rag again." So, when Killer wanted to needle me, he'd call me Rags.

When he was mad at you, he had this way of tilting his head forward and looking up at you, talking through gritted teeth, and his eyebrows would go up like the devil. That would scare the shit out of you when you were 18 years old.

He cut me my first year. I was one of the first cuts. I came in with a bad attitude. I really wasn't ready to live away from my home in Toronto. I guess he figured that out fast. But when I came back the next year, he immediately instilled this belief in me. He saw more potential in me than I did. I was a 15th round pick. I had no idea I had a chance at the NHL. But he did. I ended up playing 10 years in the NHL, but my two years in Ottawa were the best of my hockey life.

No one influenced my hockey life more than Brian Kilrea. I would go through a wall for him. And if you look at all the guys who had great junior careers in Ottawa and went on to good pro careers, that is the one thing we have in common; we would all go through a wall for Killer.

BOBBY SMITH (Ottawa 67's forward, 1975–78)

That time we hit him with the bucket of water, my train of thought in slow motion went something like this: "We're going to get this guy ... there goes the water ... Holy crap, it's the coach ... We're dead." We slammed that door so fast. He did laugh about it later. I guess it might have helped that I had about 58 goals at that point. With Brian, everyone was equal, but some were more equal than others! But he knew when to give it to you, and when to let it go.

He had these great phrases. I own the Halifax Mooseheads now, and I still find myself using them all the time. When a goalie is having a tough time in practice, he'd yell, "Be careful you don't get hit by one of those!"

He used to watch Ben Wilson eat like a horse, and say, "Do you eat until you get full, or until you get tired?"

He loved telling a guy (who he knew had skin thick enough not to get upset): "If I could make a hockey player out of you, I could make a wrist watch with a hammer."

Or, "Son, the best hockey career advice I could give you is, 'Don't quit school.'"

He was in his late 30s when I played, and he had an amazing ability to relate to these teenagers he coached. I went back 25 years later, and he had the same relationship with them. It was like he hadn't aged. I see these coaches now with their detailed systems, their "F1, F2." Killer didn't have any of that. There were no "Xs and Os" at all. But if you had the ability to be a hockey player, he was going to get it out of you.

Guys often look back at their college years as the best years of their life. I look back on my junior days with that kind of fondness. We were all trying to juggle a busy hockey schedule, high school, and trying to keep some old clunker running. It was a real golden era before we went on to the real world. One of the best parts was having Brian Kilrea leading the circus.

ALYN McCAULEY (Ottawa 67's forward, 1993–97)

A lot of my Killer stories involve Shean Donovan.

Shean must have had five real good chances a period his last year in Ottawa. More often than not, he would come screaming down the right wing and blast a shot that would miss the net and go around the rim and back out the other side. After this happened a couple of times one period, we're in the room and Killer says, "Hey, Dono, are you playing right wing for us or right defence for them? Because you are the best breakout they have!"

That same year, Shean was very close to making San Jose. He stayed with the Sharks out of camp, but was sent back to us early in the season. His first game back, between periods, Killer says, "Hey, Dono! I know the Sharks sent you back. But if it's not too much trouble, could you call and ask the general manager to ship your brain back, too? Because you left it behind."

I don't know how he came up with some of his lines. There was one player, who I won't name, who was really hunched over when he skated with the puck. So, we're doing some drills, 3 on 2s, 2 on 1s, and Killer calls us together. He says to the player, "You skate like a dog humping a pumpkin!"

I remember thinking, what mind has ever put a dog and a pumpkin together?

When you screwed up something simple, he'd say, "Anyone with an elbow and an arse hole could do that!"

Another time, Mike Sim, brother of NHL player Jon Sim, hit our goalie in the head during a practice and cut him. They had to go stitch him up. Killer wasn't happy, so he made Mike play goalie for the rest of practice, with just his regular gear on! We were firing away at the poor guy.

It was always entertaining. It took me a while to figure Killer out. The first couple of years when he was giving it to someone, I would just stare at my skates. I wasn't sure what to think. But then I started to look up, and see him give a little nod or wink to Bert before he started yelling. I realized it was mostly tongue in cheek. He never meant to be hurtful, he was just trying to stir the guys up, or loosen them up. You realized hockey was still just a game to him. He didn't take it that serious.

He would do anything for his players. I remember when my girlfriend's (now my wife) grandfather passed away. I went to Killer and told him. Not only did he give me a couple of days to go to the funeral, he handed me the keys to the Chevy Lumina he drove because he knew I didn't have a ride. That enlightened me to the person he was, how much he cared.

GARY ROBERTS (Ottawa 67's forward, 1982–85)

My junior draft year, I was 16 years old and we didn't think I had any chance of being drafted. But Ricky Curran, the agent, came to my house, and said, "You should go to the draft, I think you might get taken." I really didn't believe it, so I showed up at the draft, with long hair, wearing a lumber jacket.

Well, the 67's picked me in the second round. I go down to their table, Killer looks at me and, without a smile, all he says is, "Get a haircut, get in shape and I'll see you in September." That was it. One sentence. I was terrified. And on the way to the car, my Dad was giving me shit for not dressing properly. I left with my tail between my legs.

I was scared to death of Killer my first year. All he ever did was yell at me. I got into two fights at school, and he brought me into his office both times, threatening to send me home. He tore a strip off me.

But at the end, as I was leaving, he'd say, "So, did you win the fight?"

"Uh, yeah. I did."

"Good."

My second year, we won the Memorial Cup. I had partied too much my first year, so he called me in before the season and said, "Roberts, this is your draft year. I know you didn't behave yourself last year. So, I'm going to call you every night at 11 p.m. If you aren't home, I'm sending you home."

He never actually called, but I still took it seriously. I soon realized that if Killer yelled at you, it was a good thing. If he stopped, you were in trouble.

He left for the Islanders after he won the Mem Cup. A guy named Cliff Stewart replaced him. Cliff wouldn't allow us to swear, made us write an essay about why we wanted to play hockey, and made us go to church on Sundays and pray for wins. You imagine going from Killer to that?!? I think we went 1-13 before he was fired.

We were last place for the next year-and-a-half, which probably says more about Killer than anything else. Outside of my father, he is the most influential person in my hockey life. He had the ability to make you want it more. People say you can't teach desire. He taught me desire.

SEAN SIMPSON (Ottawa 67's forward, 1977–81)

One time, we played in London on a Tuesday night, and there was a huge snowstorm. We used to always eat at this place right off the 401 in Port Hope called Beeston's. I think it's a Harvey's and a Swiss Chalet now. But somewhere outside Oshawa, a tractor-trailer had jackknifed, and the highway was completely blocked. We had played a hockey game, we hadn't eaten, and we were stuck for hours. Most teams would be moaning and groaning, but not us. These flashing lights from a truck in front of us were beaming through the bus, and it looked like some TV show set. So, Jim Ralph grabbed the mic, and turned it into a game show. All of us, including Killer, were howling. Then, we grabbed our sticks, and went outside and played. You know how your Mom and Dad, when they're mad, say, "Go play on the 401." Well, we really did! The truck drivers were beeping their horns, loving it. We didn't get to eat until 5 a.m., and we didn't get home until 11:00. But we didn't care. That was the kind of team we had, and the kind of atmosphere Killer created. You didn't complain—you made the best out of it. You had fun.

ADAM CREIGHTON (Ottawa 67's forward, 1981–85)

We had a player named Brian McKinnon, who really liked to show he was working hard by making all these pained expressions. And every time he got hit, he'd wince like he was hurt. One day, he was doing this and Killer says, "McKinnon! You look like Lon Chaney, Man of a Thousand Faces!" That cracked us up.

The only time I really got in trouble with him was my second year when I told him I was going to quit school. He got upset. "You shouldn't do that, it's important," he said. I said, "Too late, I already did." He knew he couldn't change my mind, so he made me come down to the rink every morning at 9 a.m. I'd skate, then work out, then come up to his office and talk hockey. There were a few of us. Those were some of my favorite times with him. He didn't have to rant and rave and tear a strip off you. He'd just talk. Plus, my landlady used to pack me a lunch that could feed 10 people. So we'd pig out, and listen to Killer talk hockey.

At the end of the year, he'd always drive three or four of us back home for the summer. On the way, we'd stop and meet with all the new draft picks. He'd say to me, "When the mother and father ask you guys about school—Adam, you keep your mouth shut!" I was a good player for him, but I sure wasn't his favorite role model for education.

BERT O'BRIEN (Ottawa 67's assistant coach, 1986–2009)
It was important for a few kids on the team to have cars, to get the other players around town. If it ever came down to a decision between two kids with equal talent, well, the kid with the car might have the edge! So, once we kept a kid with a car over another kid, but about two months into the season, he wasn't working out. He walks into the office one day and says, "Coach, I heard the team takes care of our cars, and my transmission is gone. Could you get it fixed?" Killer tells him he is busy, so the kid leaves. And Killer says, "That transmission better get him to Kitchener." He didn't get traded that day, but it wasn't long before he was gone.

The first time we were retiring, we were in the deciding game of a first-round series against Peterborough. There was a home show on at the Civic Centre, so we had to play at the Robert Guertin Arena in Hull. If we lose, Killer and I are finished coaching (or so we thought). With about 1:10 to go, the Petes are leading us by a goal. Michael Peca trips a guy right in front of our bench and takes a penalty. It's the last minute, we're shorthanded, and the best player on our team is in the box. I'm thinking, "We can't win! We're done! Our coaching career is over." Killer comes down the bench and says to me, matter-of-factly, "Well, that's going to make it a little more difficult."

I couldn't believe it! I'm thinking he wants to talk strategy, and that's all he says! He was so relaxed. And what happens? Steve Washburn scores with two seconds left, Wade Simpson scores in overtime, and we win the series. And then we won the next one, too, before North Bay finally beat us out. I'll never forget that line.

That reminds me of another one. Global TV used to do a Game of the Week on Saturday afternoons. We were in Belleville, the coldest damn rink in the world. I was shivering the whole game. Anyway, we won in overtime, and when I got home, I watched the game on my beta machine— that was the latest technology back then. At one key point late in the game, they show Killer coming over and saying something to me. The commentator says, "There's Brian Kilrea going over strategy with his assistant, Bert O'Brien." Well, I burst out laughing. All he had really said to me was, "Jesus Christ, are they hanging beef in this place?"

MIKE PECA (Ottawa 67's forward, 1991–94)

I got traded to Ottawa from Sudbury at the deadline. I had just arrived when we went up to Cornwall for a game. You're nervous, all your equipment is new, you're not sure what to expect. Well, we were playing lousy and Killer says to Grayden Reid, one of the veterans, "Reider, why don't you just take off your skates and walk to the bus station? You're done with this team." Then he goes off on Brett Seguin, "Seguin, why don't you just buy a bar to save yourself some money?" I'm thinking, "What is going on here? Is this the way he always is?"

It took me a while to figure it out. My first year, I would be in the dressing room when Killer came in, and I saw veterans biting on their towels. I couldn't figure out why, but I knew that my Dad used to get my buddies and me in trouble if we laughed at the dinner table, so we would bite on our napkins when we got the giggles.

This was no different. When you get to be a veteran, sometimes Killer would come to you outside the room and say, "Look, I'm going to have to give it to you in there. Don't start laughing." He wanted to scare the rookies, and the best way to scare the rookies was to scream at the veterans. Soon, I was biting the towel, too.

He did everything for me. I had played wing my whole life until I got to Ottawa. He said right away, "You're not a winger, you're a centreman." I guess he liked the way I read the game, and the way I passed. He taught me the importance of passing off my backhand. We worked on that endlessly. It's an underrated skill, and he preached that you should pass equally off your forehand and backhand. Those little things made all the difference to me in my pro career.

The other thing is, his systems are pretty simple. So, he allowed players to develop their skills, instead of being stuck in some robotic system. I think that's why he turns out so many skilled players.

DARREN PANG (Ottawa 67's goalie, 1982–84)

I used to go down too early, and it was driving Killer nuts. He kept telling me, "Stay on your feet. Don't be like Mike Palmateer!" So, one night we're playing at home against Kingston, and this one guy comes down the left side and blows one between my legs. Then I give up another, then a third, in the exact same place. Same player, same side! Well, I don't even have to look at the bench, I know I'm being yanked. I skate to the bench and Killer is beside himself. "Pang! Stay on your !*#!ing feet!" We had these big giant plastic pucks that hung in the Ottawa Civic Centre, with the 67's logo on them. Killer says, "See those pucks up there, Pang! Those could go between your legs!"

He yelled at me again in the dressing room, but then at the end of the tirade, he says, "Put your mask on and get out there for the second!" As mad as he was, as bad as I was, he wanted me back in there. We end up winning the game, and when I read the paper the next day, he says nothing about the goals against. He just says, "We don't win that game if Pang doesn't make that big save in the second." I go from feeling awful to feeling like a million bucks. That is what makes him the greatest coach in the world.

Of course, the next day in practice, he huddles us up on the ice and says, "Pang! If you go down once in this practice, you don't play for three weeks!"

After practice, he says to me, "Pang! Did you give up one goal between your legs in that practice?"

"Not one, Coach. But I gave up a whole bunch on the ice."

"I don't care!"

He didn't have to do what Eddie Shore did, and hang the rope around my neck and tie it to the crossbar. I got the point, and he never had to tell me again. I became a better goaltender from that point on. It was a turning point in my career.

BRYAN TROTTIER (New York Islanders forward, 1975–90)

"Asses and eyeballs! Asses and eyeballs!"

That's what Killer would always tell us on the forecheck. "If you see their asses, let's pressure like hell! If you see their eyeballs, we'll just send one." I never forgot that. The other thing I remember about him from his two years with the Islanders was that he always brought this little sandwich bag on the bus. No matter where we were going on a road trip, Killer would always have this little snack bag, with a sandwich, or a piece of cheese. His wife would always pack him a snack. He would get ribbed about it, for sure. But he didn't care. He could rib right back with the best of them.

I sat right behind him on the bus, and would listen to all his stories about Eddie Shore and his days in the minors. I was in disbelief. It was like slave labor back then! And I was always full of questions, and he would answer all of them. He gave me a lot of time, and I loved the guy.

MARK EDMUNDSON (Ottawa 67's forward, 1992–95)

I remember Brian coming to our house in London before the draft. I was a little intimidated—he had such a tough reputation. But he sat down with me and my family and he was an absolute gentleman. My family took a liking to him right away, and I was thrilled to be drafted eighth overall to Ottawa in 1992.

The 67's used to always do a big early season swing through Windsor, Guelph and Detroit. I was about 10 games into my junior career when I played my first game in my hometown. My Dad bought about 80 tickets. Everybody was there. Now, I had gone to the same high school where most of the London Knights go. In fact, I was dating the captain of the school's cheerleading squad. And, put it this way, most of the players on the Knights wanted to date her. So, in the first period, there's a melee and this guy Troy Sweet grabs me and basically says, "I want your girlfriend and I'm going to kill you!" And he came pretty close. He beat the tar out of me. Uppercuts, over/unders. I didn't even get a punch in. My girlfriend and my little niece and nephew were in the stands crying. I had two ice bags over my eyes in the penalty box. I couldn't even see.

Obviously, I was feeling pretty awful. Then Killer comes into the dressing room after the period and says, "Eddie, great job! That guy hurt his hands! He's not coming back! You got him out of the game! Great job!"

I was laughing. He found a way to make me feel better.

I've heard how a father told Killer, "I gave you a boy and you gave me back a man." For me, it was more, "I came in a student and I left a teacher." I've coached senior hockey, I've coached in hockey schools, and I've tried to pass on the same things he taught me.

I've tried to instill in players the need to have passion, but still be humble. I tell them, "When you come to the rink, give me 100 per cent. I won't ask for anything more." That was what Killer taught me. I've tried to teach the same thing. I loved the guy. Still do.

LARRY MAVETY (Kingston Frontenacs general manager, former Belleville Bulls GM)

We've been friends since the Eddie Shore days in Springfield. When they were going on strike, I was playing in Port Huron, and Killer called me to say, "If Shore calls you to come replace us, don't come!" I had been there a bit before, but as a black ace. Shore didn't like me. At my first training camp, he yelled at me because he didn't like the way I stepped on the ice!

Killer did a lot for me. When we [Belleville] came into the league, most of the guys who called you just wanted to take advantage of you, to rape you of players. Killer wasn't like that. He helped me a lot. I would phone him and ask for advice on players.

And the trades we made were fair. He was never out to fleece me.

We had some great times. One time they beat us in Ottawa, and we went out after. I ended up staying at his place, sleeping on the couch. He lent me his car the next day to drive home. I pull into practice in Belleville driving this car with a big 67's logo on the side, the day after they beat us! And he had taken a picture of me sleeping with his little fluffy dog on my chest. He got good mileage out of that.

It usually wasn't fun playing against his teams. He knew how to win. One night, we were up on them by a bunch of goals . . . five or six . . . and they came back and won on a fluke shot from centre in the last minute. I went to the dressing room, steaming, and the door was locked. So I kicked it and broke my foot. Killer's fault.

ANDREW CASSELS (Ottawa 67's forward, 1986–89)

I chewed tobacco, but Killer never knew. That was one thing he was totally against. He thought it was disgusting. But in my years there, he never found out. I'd go up to the front of the bus and ask Tank for a cup. Killer would say, "Get Andrew a cup, Tank!" He had no idea it was to spit my dip in. So I was playing in Montreal early in my NHL career, and I came back to Ottawa for a party they were having for one of the billets. I walk in with a dip and Killer says, "When did you start that?" I say, "I did it the whole time I played for you!" Oh, was he mad. He says, "I would have traded you if I knew!" I say, "No, you wouldn't have!" He couldn't believe I had done it my entire career in Ottawa. I ran into him again the next summer at the Ex and he started yelling at me again about it. I think he felt like his son had deceived him. It showed you how much he cared.

It's the times he was really mad I remember most, because sometimes it was so funny. This one game, he came into the room and was just fuming. This was the worst I had ever seen him. He was clenching his fists and strutting back and forth. We had this wooden table in the room with a big jug of Gatorade on it. Killer was so mad, he punched it, thinking he was going to knock it over. But this thing was totally full, and weighed a ton. It didn't budge, and you could just hear the sound it made on his knuckles.

He just walked out and you could see him shaking his hand in pain as he left. We were all trying so hard not to bust out laughing.

SEAMUS KOTYK (Ottawa 67's goalie, 1997–2001)

The very first road trip of my junior career, we were playing in Peterborough on a Thursday night. So Killer comes up after Wednesday practice and says, "Don't worry about having your landladies make you supper tomorrow. I'm going to have chicken and potatoes on the bus." That sounded like a pretty fancy meal to us. So, we get on the bus and on every second seat there is a bucket of Kentucky Fried Chicken, fries and cole slaw. I think it was Matt Zultek who said, "What's this?" Killer yells, "What's the matter, you don't like chicken?" Then he says, "And don't even think about touching the cake at the back, that's for my over-agers!" Those were the days you got a McCain Deep 'n' Delicious Cake when you ordered a bucket at KFC. That was his dessert for the veterans. That game in Peterborough, all the rookies were doubled over with grease cramps. Killer wasn't exactly a dietitian, but he always made sure we were fed!

He loved to give it to some guys. The year we won the Memorial Cup, we had this player named Jonathan Boone, who really struggled to get into the line up. He didn't play much at all. But I do remember he took Killer out a couple of times at practice, knocked him over by mistake. So, we were doing this flow drill one time, and Boone comes in and scores on me. Well, Killer blows his whistle and calls us all together at centre ice. We didn't know if he was going to yell at us or what. Then he asked me to go get the puck out of the net. He says, "Guys, let's congratulate Jonathan Boone! He just scored his first OHL goal!" Maybe he was getting even for the times Jonathan had taken him out. We howled.

But the truth is, no one cared more about his players. We were in Sarnia once, and Ben Gustavson took a puck in the face and had to leave the game. We come in to the room after the period, and Ben is sitting there with a cage on his helmet, ready to go back out. Killer looks at him and gets choked up. Killer knew how badly we wanted to play for him. He understood that Ben didn't have to go out and play, nor was he asked. It was something Ben wanted to do, something we all wanted to do. And you could see how much Killer appreciated that.

MIKE FUTA (LA Kings scout, former Owen Sound general manager)

One night, we were in Kitchener together, and Killer always loves to go for wings after. But this night, we go to the Charcoal Grill beside the Radisson Hotel. Now, this is a $45 steak place, and that's not really Killer's scene. So, he pulls out the menu, and he's looking at it, desperately trying to find a chicken wing. The waitress comes over, and he goes, "What the heck is a chicken . . . sa-tie? Is that wings? 'Cause all I want is wings."

Well, there are no wings, so he orders the chicken satay, and it comes out, and the look on his face is priceless. "That's a chicken? What are these sticks?" I was just dying.

Killer knows what he wants, that's for sure.

He is truly one of the great men in hockey. And no one makes me laugh harder.

JIM FOX (Ottawa 67's forward, 1977–80)

My first year was the year after they had gone to the Memorial Cup in Vancouver. We had some unbelievable players. The top line was Bobby Smith, Steve Payne and Tim Higgins. Killer loved offensive hockey. He had no time for boring, sit-back-and-defend hockey. So, we're playing in Peterborough one night and they play the exact opposite system. They play very defensively. From the first shift, they decide to shadow Smitty's line. As soon as Killer realizes this, he calls time-out and calls us all to the bench. He tells all three guys on that line to stand at the Petes' blue line and not move.

So they do, and the three Peterborough guys stand right next to them. So the two teams basically played 2-on-2 hockey! There was the odd whistle, but this kept going all period. Smitty's line never came off, and the Petes' just stayed there with them. Killer was fighting for his brand of hockey. He was standing behind the way he wanted the game to be played. It was something to see. I think we lost the game, but he made his point.

Killer meant everything to me. After my second year of junior, I was eligible to be drafted, but there were only six rounds then, and I didn't get picked. There weren't many rules back then as far as free agency, so I could have signed with an NHL team if one wanted me.

Killer comes to me and says, "I have an agent friend, Larry Kelly. He can help you. And I can call Don Cherry (who was coaching Colorado at the time) and he will sign you. He was putting me ahead of the 67's. I had a year left in Ottawa, but he wanted me to get to the NHL. He always put his players' lives first. And in turn, that's why we played so hard for him. We loved him.

When Brian's Mom died, they had a wake for her. The entire team was there, and we didn't leave until 5 a.m. And we had a game that next night. That would never happen today. But the hockey team was part of his family. And his family was ours.

STUMP (Gary Craig, Ottawa 67's equipment man)

Killer and I started playing baseball and hockey together when we were kids. When my Dad kicked me out, the Kilreas let me live with them. They were fantastic people.

I would get in fights and get thrown in jail. Killer's Dad, Jack, would always bail me out. My fighting days are done. I'm six days younger than Killer. I've had both knees operated on, my shoulder, my lower bowel, my heart. I had a four-bagger in my chest. No more scraps for me.

Killer was never a fighter, on or off the ice. He didn't take any crap from anyone, but he wouldn't start trouble. And he often kept me from starting it. He did so much for me, letting me go on all those bus trips with the 67's. He made me feel like part of the team.

DOUG WILSON (Ottawa 67's defenceman, 1974–77)

My last year of junior, I was 19, and I tore cartilage in my knee and was out for a while. I hadn't been cleared to play yet, so Killer had me over one night just to sit around and talk hockey. We had a few, too. He let me stay at his place. I don't think I even slept. We get to the rink the next day for an afternoon game, and a couple of the players are sick. So Killer asks me if I want to dress. Well, I haven't even been cleared to play yet!

"Don't worry," he says. "Just sit on the bench." Of course, I should have known better. I played 20 minutes.

I admire Killer more than anyone in the world outside my family. He is a teacher of life. He treated us like men, taught us how to treat other people, taught us about honesty—he was brutally honest. The decisions I make now, in hockey and life, are greatly influenced by what he taught me.

My Dad was in the Air Force, and he and Killer got along great because they were both very honest, straightforward people. My father passed in 1982 when he was just 52. Killer has been like a second father to me.

BRIAN CAMPBELL (Ottawa 67's defenceman, 1995–99)

Killer always enjoyed the trips everywhere we played, but there was one town and arena he didn't like as much. I won't say which one. But we were playing them in the playoffs one year, and I think we won in their barn, and the next two games were at home. If we won both, we'd wrap up the series. So, he gets on the bus, and walks back to where the players are sitting and says, "If we never have to come back to this place again, I'll take you anywhere you want for dinner, and you can party till you drop." We all went nuts cheering. We won the next game, and we had a chance to wrap it up at home. He comes into the room before the game, and doesn't say anything. He just writes on the board, "Till you drop!" Best pre-game speech ever. We won. On the Monday, he took us all out for a great dinner.

The thing I admire most about him is that he treated us like adults. He respected us, gave us responsibility, and as long as you didn't cross the line, you were always treated well.

LOGAN COUTURE (Ottawa 67's forward, 2005–09)
During my first year, we were playing in Kingston on New Year's Day. We were playing awful. We fell behind 4-0. So, after the period, we expected Killer to come in and let us have it. We waited, and waited, but he didn't come in. Finally, Bert comes in and says, "Killer says he doesn't deserve to coach you, and you don't deserve to be coached, so he's going to watch instead." We weren't sure if he was joking or not, but we come out and Killer isn't there. We start playing and Derek Joslin, our captain at the time, gives me a nudge on the bench, and says, "Look over there." There is Killer, high up in the corner of the stands with a big fat bag of popcorn, watching the game.

Guys say he's intimidating, but he's really one of the nicest, funniest guys you'll ever meet.

DENNY OLSON (Springfield Indians, 1958–65)
We go back over 50 years. We were both in Detroit's system, and met at Customs, going across to the American Soo for

training camp. We've been friends ever since, and were roommates most of the time in Springfield.

We always had these little bets. First guy to 20 goals, the other guy buys dinner. We played crib for who would buy breakfast. Killer loved cards. He was a helluva poker player. I would be shaving in the morning, and he would be sitting on the toilet with a deck of cards, playing about seven different hands. He was trying to figure out what the other guys might draw when he played on the bus later. He was always thinking. That's why I was never surprised he turned out to be such a great coach. He would take everybody's money on the bus. But then we'd get to the bar, and he'd buy everyone a drink. He'd say, "What are you thanking me for? It's your money!"

Here's one more Eddie Shore story. We were in Hershey one time in the old Cocoa Inn, and Eddie's room was kitty-corner from us. Eddie was always trying to catch guys going out, so he had his room where he could open the door and see right down to the fire escape, where guys would try to sneak out. Well, the doors were really creaky in the Cocoa, so Killer and I decided to have some fun with Eddie. We kept opening our door, and then closing it, so he'd have to keep coming out to check. We peeked out and saw him prowling the hall in his blue pyjamas.

At breakfast in the morning, Eddie walks over to our table and says, "You two sleep good?" Killer was trying to keep a straight face. I say, "Yes, but I thought I saw a burglar in blue pyjamas." Eddie growls, "I wasn't the only burglar up." He had figured us out. But, you know what? He picked up our cheque. So he did have a sense of humor, once in a while.

Whenever I see Killer, we laugh about those days. My wife and I celebrated our 50th anniversary a few years back. Killer sent me a 67's sweater with "50" on the back. I'll never forget that. He was a great teammate and roommate. He's a better friend.

JAMES CYBULSKI (former Ottawa 67's public address announcer, now TSN anchor)

During my first year in college in 1993, we were assigned the task of interviewing a prominent figure in Ottawa. I immediately thought of Brian Kilrea. To any hockey fan growing up in Ottawa, he was larger than life. I remember reaching him, and trembling in fear as I spoke to him over the phone, asking for a few minutes of his time, face-to-face.

"Well, how long will you be?"

"About 10 minutes, sir."

"It better not be any longer, I've got a lot of shit to do!" Click.

Oh, my God, I was terrified. I spent the whole night trying to write down good questions. The next day, a second-year student warned me that he had been tossed out of Killer's office for asking dumb questions. On the bus ride to the Civic Centre, my heart was pounding.

I rewrote all my questions. When I finally got to his office, he took one look at me and said, "James, come with me." We walked outside, and he pulled out a hot dog bun. "Before we do this, we're gonna feed the birds."

I think he knew how nervous I was, and so he wanted to put me at ease. I wound up with a great interview and a good grade. I'm convinced it wouldn't have happened if he hadn't taken those few minutes to make idle chitchat and make me comfortable.

I would go on to become the 67's public address announcer. One Saturday afternoon in the fall of '98, the 67's were playing a home game against the Oshawa Generals. A good crowd of about 7,500 fans was on hand. It was in the third period, and Ottawa was up big, something like 7-2. When it was time to announce the 50-50 winner, the person who won was from Oshawa. The crowd started booing loudly, so I joked over the PA system, "Oh well, they have to win something!" Everyone laughed and cheered. After the game, I went downstairs to the team's dressing room and saw Brian Campbell and Nick Boynton, who both asked me if I had seen Killer. They warned me that he was not impressed with what I said. When I got around the corner, I saw him and he immediately barked, "Knock it off with that stuff! We don't need to give them any more reason to kick our butts!" He sounded furious. Then he said, "Now, sit down and have a beer." It was over, just like that.

It showed me how respectful he was in victory at all times.

TERRY MARCOTTE (CTV Ottawa sports anchor)

There are so many stories. He calls one local newspaper guy "Jeopardy," because when he asks a question, he gives you the answer, too.

One day, I go to the rink to interview one of his stars. Killer says, "Why do you want to talk to him?" I answer, "Because he's struggling." Killer goes, "Not according to him," and he skates away. Then he comes back and says, "When you talk to him, get him to show you the holes in his hands." I'm puzzled. "Holes in his hands?" "Yeah," says Killer. "Thinks he's Jesus Christ."

Another time, Seamus Kotyk is having a rough game in goal. Killer walks in to the dressing room between periods and says, "Everyone stand up and look around." All the players are confused. They have no idea what's going on. Finally Killer says, "Now anyone who finds Seamus's confidence, please give it to him. He's lost it."

I called Killer recently looking for contact info for Tim Higgins, his former star. He says, "I've got this email address, but it means nothing to me. I don't use email. Here goes. All small letters ... t higgins ... then an 'a' with some f!#*in' circle around it ..."

We tell those stories, and laugh and laugh, but there's also the human side of Killer. I was at the 67's Booster Club dinner last year when he was stepping down as coach. They read letters from fans. It made me tear up. The little things he did ... going out of his way to make people feel special. That is the side of Killer that makes him work. Yes, he's funny; yes, he's a great hockey guy; but that other side of him is the glue.

PAT HIGGINS (long-time Ottawa 67's scout)

The year Nick Boynton was drafted by Washington, and didn't sign, Nick was in a bad mood all year, and he and Killer were fighting. As we were driving to the draft in Barrie, Killer said, "I think we might have to move Nick." So Nick shows up at that draft and I pull him aside and say, "You need to talk to Killer and work this out." Nick says, "I know. I've been an idiot, I want to apologize." Nick comes over to our draft table. Now, we only have about five or six guys, while the other teams have about 12. That's just Killer's way. Nick is talking to Bert, apologizing, as Bert is marking names off our draft list. Well, with Nick distracting us, we miss marking a guy off the list, and we announce his name!

You forfeit the pick when that happens. We thought we were dead, we were all going to lose our jobs. Killer looks at us and says, "Oh well, that's one less guy we have to cut."

Killer's son Billy played junior B with me, and he also knew me through my brother Tim, so we got to be friends. When Peter Lee was coaching, Killer was scouting. So when Killer took over the team again, he needed to replace himself as a scout. He called me and asked if I would be interested. I think I was going to get $1,000 a year, and even that, Killer said, he would have to get approved by the owner, Earl Montagano. So I didn't take it for the money. But it meant a lot that Killer wanted me to replace him.

TIM HIGGINS (Ottawa 67's forward, 1974–78)

He was really superstitious. He used to keep all the coins he found in his pocket. He also had this little butt end of a stick in there. Our dressing room had one wall that was all mirrored glass. One night, he snapped on us, took everything out of his pocket and through it at the wall. There were all these coin chips permanently in the glass. It was a daily reminder for us of what might happen if we didn't give our best effort.

There were so many things he said that stay with you forever. I'll never forget his last regular season game. All the guys came in for it. We had about 30 ex-players all sitting in this one section of the stands. Well, we're watching the game and one of the poor 67's defencemen fires the puck right up the middle. The other team steals it, and they score. One of the guys, I think it was Shean Donovan, yells, "You have three choices. Get the puck off the glass, get the puck off the *!#$ing glass or get the puck off the *!#$ing glass!"

Thirty guys are laughing, and the rest of the people around us have no idea what we're talking about.

18

Time To Go

The first time I left coaching, in 1994, I did it because of my health. At the end of the year, my throat started to swell up. I kept getting worse and worse, but I wouldn't have it looked at. We were in the playoffs. I was busy.

But when the playoffs were over, I finally went over to the doctor. The nurse was my cousin, and when I walked in, she said, "Oh, my God!"

It was so swollen, I no longer had a neck. It was just face and jaw. The doctor said, "You need to get to the hospital right now. We have to operate tomorrow."

I never asked what it was. I didn't want to know. I just know that after the operation they said I was a very lucky man. So, I recovered for a couple of days, then I got shingles. I don't wish that on anyone. Boy, is it painful. I also had pneumonia and a kidney stone. All within a few months. I was falling apart.

So I walked away.

I recommended Peter Lee to coach the 67's because he was the hardest working player I'd ever coached. I told you about him earlier, firing those weighted pucks for hours after every practice. It was a natural fit—one of the best players in Ottawa 67's history coming back to coach the team.

But it didn't work. I think Peter expected everyone to work as hard as he did, but that wasn't the case. They didn't work hard for him. Peter thought they would get in great shape like he always was, but they didn't. And they'd stay out on the ice too long.

The team was struggling. So our owners, Howard and Earl, came to me, and asked me to come back because they could see the team sliding. I felt really bad for Peter. But we're friends today. I still use him as an example to my players about hard work. And he has become one of the most successful general managers in Europe.

So I went back behind the Ottawa 67's bench. And I coached 15 more seasons. Everything happens for a reason, remember?

There was no one moment that I decided to step down for good. During the 2007–08 season, I started to think about it. The Mondays were getting tougher. And the responsibility of making sure everything was done right was wearing on me.

You know, all the extra stuff that goes with coaching a team. Like crossing the border, for instance. You have to make sure everyone has their passports. I'd always prepare a list with all my players to give the officials at the border, and if we had Europeans, they would be at the top of the list. Little things like that were wearing on me.

Then we lost in the playoffs to Belleville in 2008. They were the best team in the league, but I was still disappointed. And I realized I was going to be 75, and these kids were coming here at 16. The gap was getting too big. I didn't want them hearing, "Are you with that old guy in Ottawa?" It's funny, I don't feel old. But to them, I am.

Plus, we had an assistant coach, Chris Byrne, who was waiting in the wings, and I believed he was ready to take the team.

Judy and I talked, and we both felt it was the right time to go. So I went to Jeff Hunt and told him, "Next season is going to be my last."

Jeff Hunt: *I think the first time I started to see it coming was four years earlier, when we made it to the Memorial Cup in London, and lost out to Sidney Crosby and Rimouski. Killer always had this ability to put things behind him. Give him 20 minutes, even after the toughest loss, and he'd be able to have a laugh over a beer. The last night of any season was always a great one with Killer.*

But that night in London, we went back to the hotel for beers, and Killer didn't join us. We'd had this great year, there was no shame in losing to Rimouski. But I think it was hard on him, all the commitments, all the media. A couple of days later, at the year-end banquet, we were off to one side and he said, "I think it's time." I didn't even know what he was talking about. I said, "Time for what?" He said, "To pack it in." I was shocked. We had just had this wonderful season. But he was worn out. Now, as summer went by, he recharged the batteries, and he ended up going on for four more years. But I knew that night it wouldn't be too much longer. When he told me the next time, I knew he meant it.

I didn't want to announce it until after the season was over. I didn't want to have one of those retirement tours. I just wanted to walk away quietly. But Jeff said it would be nice if the people around the province had a chance to say goodbye.

Jeff Hunt: *I told him, "You owe it to the fans in Ottawa, and the rest of the league, to let them come out and show their appreciation." I knew he would be very much against it. I told him we'd have a much better season at the gate and that it would be significant to me financially. I think that's what probably sold him. He always wanted me to do well. He always treated any expense like it was his own money. So, if it was going to help me and the 67's for him to announce this would be his last season, I knew he would never go against it.*

I called Don Cherry to ask him what he thought. Don said, "Don't do it. Everyone will want to talk to you and do interviews. You'll be bombarded all season."

But I'd been thinking a lot about it, and I said, "Don, the media people have been very good to me. I've never been misquoted. And I owe them a chance to do interviews if they want." It wasn't about fanfare for me. In my mind, it was for all the people around Ontario who had helped me during my career—the fans who had come to watch our team play in their town, the reporters who covered the team when we played there. It was for them. If they wanted to cheer or jeer, that didn't matter. I just wanted to give them the chance.

It was a great year. I never wavered, never had second thoughts. Each team did a special tribute for me. They were all very, very good to me. And I thought the kids worked as hard that year as any of my teams ever did. I felt bad for them, having to sit through all those ceremonies. But they got 40 wins, and they had to earn every one of them, because they weren't one of the top teams, talent-wise.

The last regular season game in Ottawa was really special. There were so many good friends and ex-players who came. And guys like Scotty Bowman, Brian Burke, Bryan Murray and Roy Mlakar showed up. They didn't have to come, but they did. That was a tough night. Trying to get through my speech, and recognize all the people who had helped me. Boy, it was emotional.

Jeff Hunt: *If there's one thing I remember, it's the video we made. It was put to Frank Sinatra's* My Way. *If you cared about Brian Kilrea, you couldn't help but get choked up watching it. And I think everyone in that building cared about Brian Kilrea.*

The video was unbelievable. The whole night was. The kids played great. We beat Kingston 5-2. In the room after the game, all these former players came in. A lot of them brought their wives and kids. I'll never forget it.

We played Niagara in the first round of the playoffs. It was a wild series. Every game could have gone either way. We split the first six games. Game 7 was in Ottawa. We were up 3-1 going into the third. I'm not sure what happened. Maybe nerves took over. But they scored two to tie it, and we were lucky it was only two.

Twenty seconds into overtime, Niagara got the puck off a turnover and scored. And it was over.

It was hard to lose the last game like that in your hometown. I didn't feel sorry for me, but I did for the team. They played every game knowing it was my last season. They were playing for me. I think they tried too hard. They really believed they could win it all.

Logan Couture (Ottawa 67's forword, 2005–09): *We wanted badly to win for Killer. I watched a replay of that game for the first time a few months after. It was a struggle to watch. I thought we were ready going into the third. I still don't know what happened. I don't think we had a shot for the first 12 minutes. I still wish we could have that one period back.*

I was on the ice when they scored in overtime. My first thought was, "This is my last game in junior." Then I looked over to the bench and saw Killer, and it hit me that this was it for him. There were tears from every player on that team, 16 years old to 21.

The fans stayed and applauded. They were great to me for 32 years. Sometimes fans get tired of the same old coach, same style for that long. But they always remained loyal to the Ottawa 67's.

All the players stayed on the ice. Mario Cicchillo, the coach of Niagara, held his team back to acknowledge us. They had just won a series in Game 7 in overtime, yet they stood there and patiently waited until we left. That meant a lot.

As we walked off the ice, Bert tried to go ahead of me, to give me my moment. But I said, "Hold on, Bert. You come with me." We had done this together. We were going off together.

Bert O'Brien: *You never prepare for your last game, unless it's the final game of the Memorial Cup. You always think you're going to win. It's funny, my first thought walking off the ice was, "Don't fall." The last regular season game in Kingston, we'd had a shootout so one strip of the ice was clean. My feet went right out from under me and down I went! I thought I'd broken my arm and ribs. So, as I started to walk off in Ottawa, the ice was still fresh, and I was walking really gingerly, making sure it didn't happen again. It was only 20 feet before the end door that it hit me that this was Killer's last hurrah. So I stood back. That's when he grabbed me and said, "You're coming with me."*

The press was waiting, but I wanted to see my kids first. There were lots of tears in the room. I really felt for the kids who'd been with me four years—Logan Couture, Thomas Kiriakou.

I went and did all my interviews, then we went into the room, and sat and told stories. Bert, Bobby, Stump, Tank, Jeff—they were all there. Just like always.

It wasn't like I was leaving the 67's. I was staying on as general manager. But it did feel like something was ending.

The next season was tough, at first. The team didn't play well out of the gate. And when you sit up top, you see the mistakes more clearly. And it's frustrating when there's nothing you can do. But the team started playing better, and I started to get used to being away from the bench. I go on scouting trips now with Bert. We get to watch the players of tomorrow.

So, I'm content. I enjoyed my playing days. I loved my coaching days. And now I still get to be in the game.

Hockey has given me a wonderful life. I wouldn't trade it for anything in the world. It led me to my wife. It gave me a second family—the players I've coached, who have gone on to do great things on the ice and off it. It's given me a lot of great stories.

And I'm not done yet. I have some more good tales left to tell before I'm done. Pull up a chair. Did I tell you the one about the time Stump fell asleep under the seats of the bus, and lost his false teeth?

Index